THE GUIDE TO THE JEWISH INTERNET

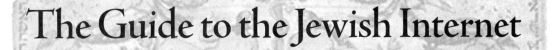

The Guide to the Jewish Internet

MICHAEL LEVIN

NO STARCH PRESS

SAN FRANCISCO

1 2 3 4 5 6 7 8 9 10—00 99 98 97 96

Trademarks Trademarked names are used throughout this book. Rather than use a trademark symbol with every occurrence of a trademarked name, we are using the names only in an editorial fashion and to the benefit of the trademark owner, with no intention of infringement of the trademark.

Credits: Image used on title page and chapter openers appears courtesy of Beinecke Rare Book and Manuscript Library, Yale University.

Publisher: William Pollock

Cover Design: Derek Yee

Interior Design: Margery Cantor

Composition: Eightball Media Group

Copyeditors: Ruth Flaxman, Carol Lombardi

Proofreader: Michele Jones

Indexer: Kimberly Lewellen, William Pollock

Editorial Assistant: Karol Jurado

Distributed to the book trade in the United States and Canada by Publishers Group West, 4065 Hollis, P.O. Box 8843, Emeryville, California 94662, phone: 800-788-3123 or 510-548-4393, fax: 510-658-1834.

For information on translations or book distributors outside the United States, please contact No Starch Press directly:

No Starch Press

401 China Basin Street, Suite 108, San Francisco, CA 94107-2192

phone: 415-284-9900; fax: 415-284-9955; info@nostarch.com; www.nostarch.com

The information in this book is distributed on an "As Is" basis, without warranty. While every precaution has been taken in the preparation of this work, neither the author nor No Starch Press shall have any liability to any person or entity with respect to any loss or damage caused or alleged to be caused directly or indirectly by the information contained in it.

Levin, Michael.
 The guide to the Jewish Internet / Michael Levin.
  p. cm.
 Includes bibliographical references and index.
 ISBN 1-886411-16-6 (alk. Paper)
  1. Internet (Computer network) 2. Computer network resources.
I. Title.
TK5105.875.I57R38   1996   96-12821
005.7'13—dc20

To my nephew, Master Harry Ethan Justus, on the occasion of his birth (http://www.neographic.com/harry).

CONTENTS

ACKNOWLEDGMENTS

THANKS ARE IN ORDER to a remarkable and wonderful group of people. First, my publisher and dear friend Bill Pollock. Bill and I went to high school and college together, which means that we've been friends for twenty years. In 1979, we co-wrote *The Subterranean Guide to Amherst College*, in which we described ourselves as "structurally unsound." I guess we're proof that even the structurally unsound can survive and thrive in the world. I'm extremely grateful to him for suggesting this book, and it has been a great pleasure to work on it with him.

I'd also like to extend my thanks to the entire team that put this book together. Ruth Flaxman and Carol Lombardi did a superb job of copyediting this book, and they went well beyond the call of duty by viewing virtually all of the sites to make sure that URLs and descriptions matched and made sense. Margery Cantor deserves enormous credit for the beautiful job of designing this book. Steve Bolinger, artist and technical wizard, produced the pages. Karol Jurado made use of her Internet prowess and captured the screens that illustrate the book. Michele Jones did her usual careful job of profreading. I mean proofreading. Kimberly Lewellen did an amazing job with the index. And the highly talented Andrea Hamel helped to create the HTML file that accompanies this volume.

Next, a special thanks to Michael Terra and the entire staff of Cybersmith, Cambridge, Massachusetts. Cybersmith is a beautiful, elegant, smart cybercafe featuring T-1 links to the Internet, good food, and a wonderful, knowledgeable staff. These folks were courteous, kind, innovative, and hard working. They always had time to help me understand what I was looking at. I had a lot of fun getting to know them as I reviewed websites for this book. If there is a Cybersmith near you, go and have a great time. If there isn't, demand one—or move.

The entire staff of the UCLA Writers Program—Linda Venis, Ray Montalvo, Christina Crews, Chad Tew, Barbara Tobolowsky,

Jonathan David, J. Greenberg, Bianca Van Deventer, and Nancy Grillo—were all extremely patient and gracious with me as I spent endless hours in their office, getting in everyone's way as I rewrote and updated the book.

Finally, highest praise and thousands of thanks to the phenomenal Jenn Burger. Jenn Burger is the hardest working individual I've ever met, and she did an excellent job with every phase of this project. She worked extremely long hours and found ingenious ways to make complex and challenging software do her bidding. Jenn is the greatest. Once again: Jenn is the greatest, and I am deeply grateful for her excellence and her commitment.

I hope you've enjoyed this book. If you have questions or comments, e-mail me at levin@nostarch.com. If you'd like us to review your site, or your favorite site, send us the URL at the same address.

Michael Levin
Santa Monica, California
September, 1996

The Heroes of the Jewish Internet

A special tip of the hat to these individuals and groups who have placed on the Internet, with great effort and with no charge, vast and wonderfully organized information, sites, lists, and more:

Matthew Album	Daniel P. Faigin
D. Powers	Tracey Rich
Steve Ruttenberg	Eliezer Segal
Eric Simon	Andy Tannenbaum
People and Computers Group	Shamash

University of Colorado Jewish Students Union

BARUCH HA-BA—
Welcome to the Jewish Internet!

The Jewish Internet is the greatest compilation of Jewish law, fact, history, opinion, news, tradition, belief, and culture since the Talmud. Never in two thousand years have Jews been so tightly woven together—and most Jews are unaware of how rich a resource it is.

Every movement of Judaism and aspect of Jewish life is represented. International Jewish organizations and individual Jews alike have equal access—even a child can surf the Internet with the ease of a Talmud scholar studying a medieval commentary.

What Is the Jewish Internet?

The Jewish Internet is the term I'm giving to all things Jewish on the Internet. There are already a few thousand "locations" on the Internet where something Jewish is happening, and more are online every day. The bad news is that the Internet can be incredibly disorganized. The best description I've heard so far is that it's like the greatest library in the world, except that all the books are in random heaps all over the floor.

The good news is that I've visited every site I could find that had any connection to Judaism or Israel or the Middle East, and I've sorted through them all in order to bring you the best, the most interesting, fun, newsworthy, exciting, or otherwise useful places on the Internet.

One of the biggest problems with the Internet today is simply the frustration and wasted time that comes from not knowing where to find the best sites. We've all been there: You've got something you want to find, so you go to Yahoo or Alta Vista or a different search engine, find a bunch of things that seem to relate to your topic. You visit them one by one … and before you know it, an hour and a half has gone by, and you're still no closer to learning anything about your topic than when you started.

Well, that's why this book exists—so that you can find exactly what you want right now. No frustration, no wasted time…and at the same time, you'll find out about Jewish Internet resources that you might not even have thought to look for.

I'll explain the technical terms in a moment, but let's start with this question: What can the Jewish Internet do for you right now?

25 Ways People Are Using the Jewish Internet Today

MEETING AND GREETING You can cruise the Internet to find all kinds of singles groups and events in practically every Jewish community in the world. You can write, read, and respond to personal ads and participate in these groups.

EDUCATION The Internet has terrific educational resources for all levels of students on every subject, from the Holocaust to Sabbath observance, to the way the Jews of Asia found their way there, to the ways Italian Jews celebrate the holidays.

SHOPPING You can find Jewish food, books, art, religious objects, and music for sale. You can see what you're buying and order it without ever getting up from your computer.

TRAVEL Up-to-the-minute information about trips to Israel, Eastern Europe, and around the globe. You can view photos of dozens of Israeli kibbutzim, read what they offer, and find out how much it all costs.

MUSIC Jewish music groups, singers, Klezmer groups, college choirs, and Israeli radio stations maintain homes on the Internet and many even offer music samples that you can listen to with your computer!

NEWS Every conceivable news outlet, from the *Jerusalem Post* and Voice of Israel Radio to your local Jewish newspaper, is on the Internet. You can read the latest from Reuters, the wire services, and other media outlets; get daily updates of Arab press reports; even hear the news broadcast directly from Israel.

RELIGIOUS STUDIES No matter what your taste in Judaism, whether Humanistic, Reconstructionist, Reform, Conservative, or Orthodox, the Internet has you covered. You'll find an entire electronic library filled with information about Judaism—from the Kaballah to the Talmud. You can read a page of the Talmud or even listen, right over your computer, to entire lectures by this century's leading rabbis.

FOOD AND WINE You'll find thousands of Jewish recipes hailing from Los Angeles to Laos; wine reviews and information on how to tour and order from Israeli vineyards; everything imaginable about keeping kosher; even updates on kosher and non-kosher products from leading Orthodox institutions.

"CHAT" ROOMS You'll find online conversations on dozens of different topics from socializing to politics to Yiddish poetry.

KID STUFF Stories, books, comic books, and educational materials for children and their parents and teachers.

ORGANIZATIONS B'nai Brith, ORT, Hadassah, they're all here. You'll find meeting times and locations and learn how to get involved.

MAGAZINES AND NEWSPAPERS You can read articles from current and back issues of magazines like *Tikkun*, the *Jewish Post of New York*, and more.

ARCHEOLOGY Visit dig sites and examine photos of discoveries, from the Dead Sea Scrolls to the Cairo Genizah. Find out how you can join digs in Israel.

ART Dozens of Jewish and Israeli artists and art galleries display their work on the Internet. View it and even buy it right from your computer.

SUPPORT AND INTEREST GROUPS Whether you're a Jew recovering from drug and alcohol addiction, concerned with intermarriage or gay issues, or simply an Israeli sports fan, you can pursue your interests here.

BUSINESS AND FINANCE Get to know many of Israel's leading banks, high tech companies, venture capital groups, and real estate firms who market themselves on the Internet.

TOUR THE JEWISH GLOBE Visit Jewish communities in dozens of North American cities, and in Europe, Israel, Africa, South America, India, the former Soviet Union, and Southeast Asia. Learn their histories, traditions, and current affairs.

TAKE A COURSE … ONLINE! Many colleges and universities around the world offer courses via the Internet. Study Judaism, Israel, Hebrew, and the Holocaust without leaving your chair.

YIDDISH Find Yiddish literature, poetry, history, and culture, online. Visit the Jewish *Forward* and the "Virtual Shtetl."

ISRAELI POLITICS Many Israeli political parties host Internet locations with position papers, articles, news briefs, names, and addresses. Many think tanks and political organizations in Israel, the United States, and Europe also offer their take on Middle East affairs.

HAVE FUN There are lots of goofy places to visit on the Internet. You can meet the extremely sexy hostess of Israel's *Wheel of Fortune.* You can "Surf the Net with Lew the Jew." You can enter contests, read jokes, and best of all, you can put your own stuff up for other people to read, too.

DOWNLOAD HEBREW FONTS You can teach your computer to read Hebrew with free software; check out the Software section of this book or go directly to one of these two websites: http://www.reshet.com/hebrew.htm or http://www1.snunit.k12.il/snunit/heb.hmtl/ and you'll get all the information you need.

SPORTS Find out what's happening in Israeli sports—football and basketball stats, schedules, and archives.

COLLEGE PROGRAMS Find out exactly what Jewish studies offerings are available at colleges and universities around the world.

RESEARCH Academics, scholars, and students can conduct serious research by means of libraries and archives around the world.

The good news is that this is all happening now. And if you have a computer but you're not already tapped in, it won't cost a fortune to join in the fun. I promise I won't throw any technical terms at you without explaining them. This is a book for people who don't necessarily have advanced degrees in computer engineering. I certainly don't.

Into ... Cyberspace

The Jewish Internet's six most important resources are:

THE WORLD WIDE WEB This is the fastest-growing and most exciting part of the Internet, and it's where most people spend most of their time when they go online. That's a sample of what a webpage looks like on the right.

The Web is a worldwide network of computers consisting of hundreds of thousands of "websites." Each website offers various webpages, composed of text, photos, sound, diagrams, animations, or whatever else the site's author wishes to show you. B'nai Brith has a website. So does 10-year-old Jeremy Glasser of Twin Oaks, Michigan. The B'nai Brith website is professionally designed and details the organization's history, names and addresses of key officers, recent issues of publications, and much more. Jeremy designed his own webpage and it has pictures of his family, his temple, and his Little League team. Anyone can put up a webpage and if you're connected you can access it.

The Web is a particularly vibrant place because webpages often have electronic links to other websites. These links appear on the webpages as clickable pictures, buttons, other images, or simply underlined and highlighted text. You use your mouse to click on the link and boom. You are instantly transported to another area of the webpage you're visiting or you're sent off to someone else's webpage. Beam me up, Scotty.

For example, if you click on the word "Services" on B'nai Brith's webpage your screen will be filled with information about B'nai Brith's services. If you click the name Jessica on Jeremy's page your screen will fill with a picture of Jeremy's sister Jessica, ice skating.

Similarly, links to "Related Sites" or something similar will probably bring you to other, related websites. For example, B'nai Brith lists other Jewish organizations, while Jeremy lists his friends, each with their own websites, too. Then, click on the name of one of those other sites and you'll probably go there. Get it? Websites and links. In fact, some websites are simply lists of other websites!

The first page you see when you reach a website is called its *home page*. At the bottom of each webpage you'll probably find the word "home." If you click on "home," you'll probably end up back at the site's home page.

GOPHER MENUS Sounds like an odd name for a computer thing, unless you went to the University of Minnesota, whose sports teams are called the Gophers. Students at the U of M designed Gopher and named it after their university mascot. Gophers on the Internet act just like the animal—they burrow through the Internet and dig stuff up.

Gophers are menu-based tools for finding information on the Internet. For example, a gopher menu connecting all the English libraries in Israel allows you to search the holdings of, say, Hebrew University in Jerusalem or the Technion in Haifa, right from your home computer. It's amazing.

INTERNET RELAY CHAT (IRC) IRC allows you to communicate instantly in a virtual "chat room" with a group of people, all typing into their computers just like you. Chat rooms are infamous as pick-up spots for lonely hearts, married and otherwise. There are also thematic chat rooms with topics like Israeli politics, Jewish culture, food, and the like.

MAILING LISTS Internet mailing lists are essentially e-mail clubs with a theme or topic that anyone can join. Topics may include Reform, Conservative, or Reconstructionist Judaism; Holocaust studies; or the military history of World War II. You join a mailing list by sending a brief message to it with a request to join. Then, automatically, you will receive via e-mail all the correspondence from all of the list's members about that topic. You can also contribute your own thoughts to the list.

By the way, mailing lists vary in quality and usefulness. Don't join too many at once or you may be deluged with hundreds of messages daily.

ELECTRONIC MAIL, OR E-MAIL You can communicate computer-to-computer via e-mail, which is simply a message that you type into your computer and send electronically. The nice part is that you never pay long distance fees for e-mail, even if you e-mail someone in Israel or, Hong Kong. You don't need to lick any envelopes either.

NEWSGROUPS Newsgroups are similar to mailing lists except that mailing lists automatically send their members' contributions to each member's e-mail address, while newsgroups keep their messages in a file that you can read and search through whenever you like. Newsgroups have names like alt.judaism.conservative or soc.Israeli.dancing.

> For more help with Internet basics, check out *Dr. Bob's Painless Guide to the Internet* by Bob Rankin (No Starch Press, $12.95, 800-420-7240) **NOTE**

So there you have it—the six most important ways by which information and opinion are disseminated along the Internet.

How Do I Get Started?

You need a computer—either an IBM-PC or compatible or a Macintosh. If you don't want to buy a new computer that's okay, but do get one that's no more than a couple of years old. (That way you can be sure that it will run fast enough.) You need Internet software too. This might be proprietary Internet software built in to the software provided by commercial services like America Online (800-827-6364),

CompuServe (800-609-1674), or Prodigy (800-PRODIGY), or a package like Netscape. If you want the easy way, start with one of the commercial services and use their Internet connection. They all offer a free startup account with a few free hours. Alternatively, contact one of the local Internet service providers you'll probably find listed in one of those free local computer newspapers. Or call Netcom at (800-NETCOM1) to get started.

You need a modem. A modem is a piece of hardware that plugs into your computer and connects to your telephone line. Most new computers come with built-in modems. Modems run at varying speeds measured in bps (bits per second). The faster your modem (the faster ones have the higher numbers—28.8 is faster than 14.4 which is faster than 9600), the faster you'll be able to cruise the Internet. Get the fastest modem around.

Now your computer is ready to go except for your link to the Internet. That link comes from a *service provider*.

Service providers come in two flavors: Those dedicated only to providing you with an Internet connection (companies like Netcom, Pipeline, and others), and those that offer an Internet connection as part of the rest of their services (like America Online, Prodigy, CompuServe, and recently the Microsoft Network). This last group offers a very good, user-friendly way to get to know the Internet. Each offers e-mail, an Internet connection, chat rooms, and lots of other bells and whistles. And each has some sort of free startup offer that lets you try their service for a short time before you have to pay a monthly or hourly fee. (Microsoft Network only runs under Microsoft's Windows 95 operating system.) Use these services as a jumping off point to the Internet and then, if you like the Internet, switch to one of the dedicated Internet service providers, which are likely to offer a much better deal.

Don't just sit there. Let's surf.

CHAPTER ONE

ARCHEOLOGY

DIGGING OUT INFORMATION about archeological discoveries used to be as time-consuming as digging antiquities out of the ground. Not anymore. This section of the *Guide to the Jewish Internet* alone will make you glad you spent all that money on your beautiful color screen. These web-sites and gopher menus take you to digs throughout the Middle East and offer you maps, photos, and information. You can search for archeological sites by region, view 14,000 year old fragments of Hebrew and Jewish literature from the Cairo Genizah, and peruse fascinating images of the Dead Sea Scrolls. What an incredible merger of ancient history with new technology.

Warning: you might get lost for centuries.

ArchNet

http://www.lib.uconn.edu:80/ArchNet/ArchNet.html

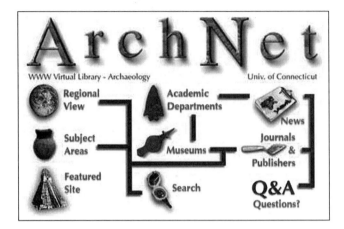

A splendid website, connecting everything to do with archeology. You can get lost for a long time in this site. Some of it has to do with Israel, but the site covers the whole world. You dig? You can search by region, by topic, or by academic department. For example, if you click on "regions" you'll get a map of the world; click on any part of the map and you'll get a long list of links to related sites. I clicked on Israel and got a list of ancient Near East resources from the University of Chicago. These include a 3-D reconstruction of an Egyptian mummy, ancient synagogues in the Holy Land, and the Ancient Palestine gallery at the museum of the University of Pennsylvania.

Berkeley Tel Dor Expedition

http://www.qal.berkeley.edu/~teldor/

This inviting home page of the UC Berkeley excavations in Tel Dor makes you feel like you're a part of the dig. The people who constructed this website obviously have a great deal of affection for their dig site, and they give you so much historical background that it's hard not to share their enthusiasm. Volunteers are welcome and their role is spelled out in depth. You'll also learn about side trips to Jerusalem and beyond. The history section and the bibliography make this a terrific website. More pictures would make it an all-star website.

Cairo Genizah

http://www.cam.ac.uk/Libraries/Taylor-Schechter/Introduction.html

A century ago, archeologists discovered a cache of 140,000 fragments of Hebrew and Jewish literature, all of it 1,000 years old, in a Cairo synagogue. This treasure trove of ancient Hebrew is called the "Genizah," meaning "storehouse" in Aramaic.

Cambridge University scholars have placed stunning color photographs of examples of the discovered manuscripts online. You can view them at this elegant and descriptive website.

Colby College in Israel

http://www.colby.edu/rel/Israel.html

Colby College's digs in Israel, featuring text and articles on glassware from Sephoris, an ancient center of Talmud study and a market town located in the lower Galilee region of Israel. For 15 centuries, glassmakers practiced their craft here. Colby's archeologists have been discovering and cataloging all kinds of different bottles, cups, window glass, and jewelry and thus learning about Jewish life from 200 B.C.E. through the 13th century C.E. Attractive color photographs round out this informative website.

The Dead Sea Scrolls

http://sunsite.unc.edu/expo/deadsea.scrolls.exhibit/intro.html

Psalms Scroll (Tehillim); courtesy of the Israel Antiquities Authority

Photos of the scroll fragments, English translations, and historical background on one of the most exciting archeological discoveries ever made, from the exhibit at the Library of Congress. Learn how the scrolls were found, what they contain, why they matter so much to Jewish history, and what they tell us about ancient Judaism.

The Dead Sea Scrolls, continued   RECOMMENDED

http://unixware.mscc.huji.ac.il/~orion/orion.html

The Dead Sea Scrolls, found by a shepherd boy in a cave at Qumran near the Dead Sea in 1947, are the most important source for information about Judaism and the times in which Christianity was founded. You can find an informative overview, with links to relevant Dead Sea Scroll websites, at the Hebrew University's Orion Center for Study of the Dead Sea Scrolls. Mostly text; some pictures. For history buffs and for anyone who wants to broaden his or her knowledge of Jewish history.

Hershel Shanks

http://www.netrail.net/~sidel/reviews/shanks.html

A brief interview with Hershel Shanks, publisher of, among other things, the *Biblical Archeological Review,* on the occasion of its 20th anniversary. Shanks, according to the website, "has changed the face of publishing in Biblical archeology." He played a large role in the campaign to get the Dead Sea Scrolls out of the hands of a few selected scholars and available to all. Why are more Christians than Jews interested in Biblical archeology? You'll find Shanks's interesting theories here.

Israel Archeology Gopher

gopher://israel.nysernet.org:70/11/israel/iis/ark

A rcheology gopher menu with a wide variety of topics related to ancient Palestine, Jerusalem, and current dig sites throughout the Middle East.

Links to Archeological Websites

http://rome.classics.lsa.umich.edu/welcome.html

O ver 300 links to ancient Greek, ancient Roman, and Middle Eastern archeological websites. Examples: field projects, museums, newsgroups, mailing lists, FTP sites. Topics include Oriental studies, the Akkadian language, and tons more. Fascinating for anyone with an interest in the ancient world.

Palestine, via University of Pennsylvania

http://staff.feldberg.brandeis.edu/~jacka/ANEP/ANEP.html

This University of Pennsylvania site takes you, with pen and camera, on a grand tour of Palestine's history. Stunning photos of archeological treasures. Sections on what they wore, arts and crafts, worship, funeral rites, food, industry, warfare—how Jews lived 3,000 years ago. Definitely worth checking out.

The Semitic Museum, Harvard University

http://scunix3.harvard.edu/~peabody/museum_semitic.html

The Semitic Museum at Harvard offers captivating photos from digs in Israel and elsewhere in the Middle East. The museum sponsors an annual dig in the port city of Ashkelon and posts at its website views of the dig as well as photos from current exhibitions. When I visited the site, I was rewarded with some amazing photos of the tombs of the pharaohs in Egypt.

Shikhin

http://www.colby.edu/rel/Shikhin.html

Visit the ancient biblical site of Shikhin at this website. Text, outstanding photographs, and maps. I go crazy looking at all this old stuff.

CHAPTER TWO

AROUND THE UNITED STATES

THIS IS A THRILLING FEATURE of the Jewish Internet. You can visit Jewish communities, synagogues, community centers, YMHAs, and more, across the United States. The Bible commands, "Uforatza," which means, "And you shall spread out!" And we have. Jews, obviously, live in every part of the country, but never has it been easier—or even possible, for that matter—to see how we live in all these places.

Many of these sites are very much the same, with slight variations in quality of design and quantity of local links. They offer a cover page with ties to different aspects of city life—like congregations, restaurants, and service groups. Some of the sites have singles pages; some of them (very few) have something unique, like the Southwest Jewish archives or the Dallas text seminar.

Boston, Massachusetts

http://www.shamash.nysernet.org/places/boston/index.html

Jewish Boston Online is a comprehensive guide to everything Jewish in the Boston area: synagogues and temples, restaurants, Jewish community centers, the Combined Jewish Philanthropies.

Brooklyn, New York

http://www.inx.net:80/~mzr77chp/

Hum the *Dragnet* theme and do your best Jack Webb imitation as you cruise for crime in Crown Heights. True life adventures of the multilingual community protection group; distur-

bances to the peace described in breathless prose. You'll feel as though you're in the patrol car, bringing safety and justice to the local Chasidic community.

Dallas, Texas

RECOMMENDED

http://www.ncc.com/dvjcc/

Put on your 10-gallon yarmulke, saddle up, and drop in on the Dallas Virtual Jewish Community Center. A model for Jewish community home pages because it's attractively designed, easy to figure out, and offers links to websites for local Jewish organizations, schools, and congregations. Also the home of the highly regarded Classic Jewish Texts Seminar. This seminar is an opportunity to learn about Jewish texts that you can study with your friends.

Detroit, Michigan

http://www.metroguide.com/jewishweb/

Everything you need to know about the Detroit Jewish community, with a singles page that spans the Jewish world.

Los Angeles, California

http://www.jewishla.com/

The home page of the L.A. Jewish Federation provides an annotated directory of service organizations, an online story for children, and more.

Maui, Hawaii

http://www.aloha.net/~bigrich/mjc.html

The Maui Jewish congregation's home page. The question is not, "Why do Jews live on Maui?" The question is, "Why don't we all move there?"

New Mexico

http://www.swcp.com/~thelink/

The Link, New Mexico's Jewish newspaper online. Get to know the Jews of Albuquerque, Santa Fe, and Taos. Lots of local and international links to Jewish organizations, congregations, and services.

Northern California

http://www.jewish.com:80/bk960308/pagehome.htm

Everything you can imagine about Jewish life in the San Francisco Bay area. Vast and complete. Activities, classes, congregations, news, and lots of personal ads, too.

Philadelphia, Pennsylvania

http://www.libertynet.org/~exponent/index.html

The *Jewish Exponent*, Philadelphia's Jewish newspaper, offers information and links to other Philadelphia Jewish sites. Scan "A Guide to Jewish Philadelphia"; locate Jewish organizations, media, and cultural institutions; find out about religious life; and more.

Pittsburgh, Pennsylvania

http://www.sgi.net/kmrbbyo/

Greater Pittsburgh's Jewish community makes its home page here. Events and more.

Portland, Oregon

http://www.teleport.com/~smjc/

The home page of the South Metro Jewish community, which views itself as "geographically and culturally distant" from Portland.

Queens, New York, YM and YWHA

http://users.aol.com/cqueensy

A resource-rich community center, the central Queens, New York, YM and YWHAs website can give other community center planners ideas on programming and services. My late grandfather, Emil Levin, helped found the Y, and he'd be pretty impressed to see it on the Web.

St. Thomas, U.S. Virgin Islands

http://www.usvi.net/caribcat/hebrew.html

Vivian Williamson-Bryan takes "a break from the beach" to set forth the 200-year history of Jews on St. Thomas. Text; photos of the astonishingly beautiful synagogue in Charlotte Amalie, the main city; and links to CaribCat, a Caribbean website offering information on rental villas "up to $8,000 a day."

Tucson, Arizona

http://www.tucson.com/JewishFed/JewishFed.html

Meet the 20,000-member Jewish community of Tucson, Arizona, at their website. Be sure to visit the Bloom Southwest Jewish Archives, a historical record of Jewish settlement in the American Southwest.

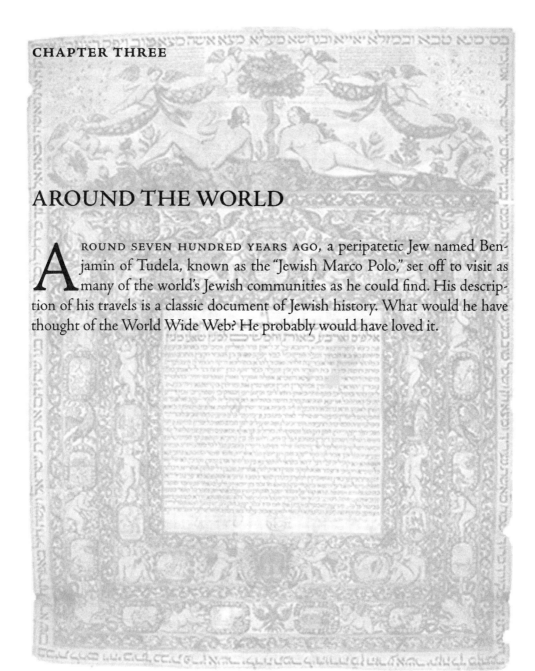

CHAPTER THREE

AROUND THE WORLD

AROUND SEVEN HUNDRED YEARS AGO, a peripatetic Jew named Benjamin of Tudela, known as the "Jewish Marco Polo," set off to visit as many of the world's Jewish communities as he could find. His description of his travels is a classic document of Jewish history. What would he have thought of the World Wide Web? He probably would have loved it.

Asia

http://www.kashrus.org/

This is an outstanding website. Learn all about Asian Jewry —essays, information, and a mailing list. All written with sensitivity and love. And a vast collection of extraordinary kosher Asian recipes. The Web at its best. From Asian-American Kashrus Services.

Australia

http://www.tmx.com.au/join/joinhome.htm

As large and diverse as all Australia, the "electronic voice of the Australian Jewish community" offers vast amounts of information and opinion about Jewish life down under. Read back issues of their newsletter, learn about Jewish studies in Australia, search a directory of Jewish organizations in Victoria, learn about Australia's community of Russian Jews, tour the Jewish Museum of Australia, and much more. Well worth a visit.

Birobidhan, Former Soviet Union

http://www.f8.com/FP/Russia/Abiro.html

Josef Stalin designated a far-off corner of what was the southeastern Soviet Union as a homeland for Jews; 40,000 or 50,000 Jews took him up on the offer. Some of them left to avoid the miserable conditions; others remained. Today the Jewish community in Birobidhan, north of the Chinese border, is having a revival. Visit them here.

Brazil

http://www.cs.huji.ac.il/~izar/samba.html

Visit your brothers and sisters from Brazil at their home in Israel. Learn about samba, capoeira—a Brazilian martial art—and other aspects of Jewish-Brazilian culture.

Canada

gopher://gopher.oise.on.ca/11/resources/list.archs

The Canadian Jewish Historical Society provides its gopher menu here.

Ethiopia

http://www.cais.net:80/nacoej/index.html

A gain, outstanding. The Internet at its best. Extremely well written and well designed guide to Ethiopian Jewry, featuring history, maps, recipes, Jewish law, and a wide variety of customs and traditions. You will be fascinated. Highly recommended.

Europe

gopher://israel.nysernet.org:70/11/ejin

The European Jewish community takes center stage on this gopher menu.

Europe, continued

http://www.ort.org/communit/ecjc/start.htm

The European Council of Jewish Communities, with member organizations throughout Europe, monitors the status of European Jewry and plans conferences about same.

Europe, continued

http://www.shamash.nysernet.org/ejin/

The European Jewish Information Network home page. Under construction; an idea with potential.

France

http://www.col.fr/tj/

Tribune Juive, French for *Jewish Tribune*, is the weekly magazine of Jewish France. Visit the site to order a free copy of the current issue. In French. Hey, mes amis, how about a little sample online?

France, continued

http://www.iway.fr/col/

Surfez sur l'Internet with Community On Line: The Voice of the Jewish Community of France. In French, with French mailing lists, French Internet links, and French cuffs.

Italy

http://www.fastnet.it/associaz/israele/israele.htm

The Association of Friends of Israel in Italy greets you in Italian at this website.

Italy, continued

http://www.inrete.it/a1/isola.html

http:// אי.טל.יה

Italy's Jewish community's webpage, mostly in Italian. Italia, in Hebrew, transliterates roughly to "islands of the divine dew." Did you know that?

Japan

http://mai.hyg.med.kyoto-u.ac.jp/KansaiWWW/Kasher.html

Japanese words for foods. A guide to Japanese menus for the squeamish, the adventurous, and the kosher.

Japan, continued

http://mai.hyg.med.kyoto-u.ac.jp/KansaiWWW/jews_pigs.html

Japan for Jewish travelers.

Manchester, England

http://ourworld.compuserve.com/homepages/inscon/homepage.htm

Manchester, England's Orthodox Jewish community offers a weekly "Chaifax" or commentary on the Torah portion, and news of its activities.

Montreal, Canada

http://www.webcom.com/rel/welcome.html

The Sephardic community of Montreal offers essays, information, and more in both French and English.

Moscow

http://www.glas.apc.org:80/~mali/english/communities/1.html

Russia: Eat here now. A Jewish business club in Moscow. Glatt kosher. Lenin is spinning in his nearby tomb.

So these two Russian Mafia hitmen are waiting outside this guy's apartment to kill him. He's due home at nine o'clock, but nine fifteen comes and he's still not there. The hit men are getting nervous. Nine twenty comes. Nine thirty.

Finally one of the hit men turns to the other and says, in all sincerity, "I hope nothing happened to him."

New Zealand

http://nz.com/NZ/Culture/Jewish/

Greetings to you from New Zealand's 3,000 Jews. You can meet them here.

Poland

http://www.igc.apc.org/ddickerson/polish-synagogues.html

Take your *zaide* (Yiddish for grandfather) on a trip down cyber-memory lane with photos of old Polish synagogues. Sensitively written descriptions accompany the excellent photographs.

Rio de Janeiro, Brazil

http://www.lookup.com/homepages/89670/home.html

Samba my best friends are Jewish: You'll really love the home page of this Brazilian Jewish youth organization…if you speak Brazilian. I mean Portuguese.

Russia: The Khazars   RECOMMENDED

http://acad.bryant.edu/~kbrook/khazaria.html

Meet the Khazars at this fascinating website. Who were the Khazars? Jews of Russian origin whose community dates from the fifth century. Very nicely done: history, a timeline, lots of extremely interesting information about a little-known aspect of Jewish history. Check it out. Produced by the Khazaria Information Centre, a group that offers no information about itself in the website but appears to be the brainchild of academician Kevin Brook. Don't miss the "Image Gallery" with its neat map and historical information.

St. Andrews, Scotland

http://www.st-and.ac.uk/~www_sa/socs/jewish/index.html

St. Andrews, Scotland's Jewish Society, offers a Bluffer's Guide to Judaism; an interview with the Chief Rabbi of Great Britain, Dr. Jonathan Sacks; and more.

St. Petersburg, Russia

gopher://gopher.jer1.co.il:70/11/comm/news/russia

Read about Jewish life in this great Russian city. This gopher menu offers the journals of the Jewish Association of St. Petersburg.

Stockholm, Sweden

http://www.algonet.se/~hatikva/judaica.html

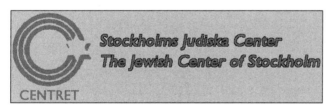

Discover the basics about the various Jewish organizations—youth, Zionist and otherwise—that call the Judaica House of Stockholm home.

Tasmania, Australia

http://jumper.mcc.ac.uk/~tas/

Tasmania, Australia, presents the Talmud Appreciation Society, with back issues of *Tasmania*, their traditionally minded online magazine for kids.

The Former Soviet Union

http://www.glas.apc.org:80/~mali/english/

News about the Jewish communities of the former Soviet Union. Fascinating, if all too brief, views of changing patterns of Jewish life.

I visited the Soviet Union in 1979 and met an American rabbi in a synagogue in what was then called Leningrad. He gave me the telephone number of a leader of the Refusenik movement in Moscow. Refuseniks were Jews who sought to leave the Soviet Union and were fired from their jobs simply because they applied for exit visas.

The rabbi told me to call the contact person from a pay phone, never from a hotel phone. When I did so, he told me to be at a particular Moscow Metro stop at three o'clock on Friday afternoon, that someone would meet me, and not to take a direct route to that station.

I followed the instructions, was met by another Refusenik, a university professor, and he took me to his home, where nine others gathered for a clandestine Sabbath dinner.

Times have changed: Practicing Judaism in Moscow, or anywhere else in the former Soviet Union, no longer reads like a Le Carré novel. When you look at the entry labeled "Jewish communities and societies in FSU [Former Soviet Union]," keep in mind how much things have changed in such a short period of time.

The Former Soviet Union, continued

http://www.glas.apc.org/~heritage/

The Jewish Heritage Society in Moscow, a group of professional and amateur Jewish scholars, is a rich resource for those interested in Russian-Jewish history. Learn about document collections inside and outside the C.I.S. (former Soviet Union) that describe Russian government laws and rulings about Judaism dating all the way back to 1792.

Turkey

http://pulex.med.virginia.edu/turkish_jews/fore.htm

Turkey welcomed Jews when Spain expelled them in 1492. But Turkish Jewish history actually goes back 2,200 years or more. Get to know your Turkish cousins at this extremely interesting and attractive website, with photos, informative text, and a transcript of a letter written around 1454 by a Turkish rabbi offering safe haven to his persecuted Spanish Jewish brothers and sisters.

Uganda

http://www.intac.com/PubService/uganda/

In the 1920s, a Jewish visitor to Uganda taught his faith to groups of interested residents of the Ugandan city of Mbale. Learn of the fascinating history of this little-known African Jewish community at this website.

United Kingdom

http://www.newmoon.co.uk/index.htm

New Moon is a monthly magazine serving the U.K. young Jewish community with articles, listings, and investigations into politics and social affairs. Its website takes great pride in being "condemned by the Jewish Establishment for championing fringe causes, including the rights of Gay Jews and the exposure of sexual and drug abuse within the Jewish community." Article excerpts and subscription information.

I have to share with you a lovely moment captured by one of New Moon's intrepid journalists: An Israeli pop singer, about to appear in London, told the reporter, apparently in a straight-faced manner: "I completely respect Madonna, but we're very different."

Actually, I could make the same statement myself.

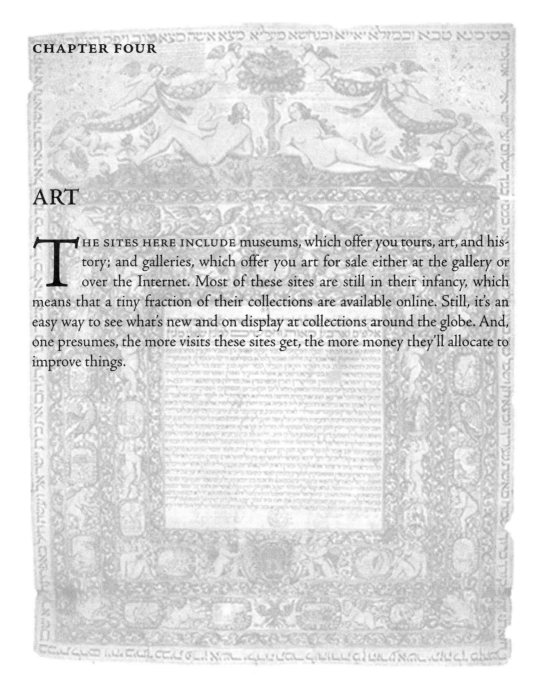

CHAPTER FOUR

ART

THE SITES HERE INCLUDE museums, which offer you tours, art, and history; and galleries, which offer you art for sale either at the gallery or over the Internet. Most of these sites are still in their infancy, which means that a tiny fraction of their collections are available online. Still, it's an easy way to see what's new and on display at collections around the globe. And, one presumes, the more visits these sites get, the more money they'll allocate to improve things.

Ben Uri Gallery, London

http://www.ort.org/links/benuri/home.htm

The Ben Uri Gallery of London presents at its website artwork related to Jewish holidays and information about those holidays.

Chagall Windows
RECOMMENDED

http://www6.huji.ac.il/md/chagall/chagall.html

A page dedicated to the glorious Chagall windows, 12 gorgeous windows of stained glass representing the 12 sons of Jacob and the 12 tribes of Israel, by the great Russian-Jewish artist Marc Chagall, located at the Hadassah Hebrew University Medical Center in Jerusalem. Stunning. Click on each window and be transported to a larger version of it. Images are downloadable. A great educational site.

Chavi Feldman Judaica Art Gallery

http://www.io.org/~yfeldman/chavi.htm

View and order the art of Jerusalem artist Chavi Feldman, who specializes in paper-cutting and ketubot.

Colors of Jerusalem

http://www.ix.co.il/colors/intro.htm

This Jerusalem gallery offers art by Russian, Ethiopian, and Israeli immigrants. The gallery owners take great pride in the fact that their artists risked their lives for their artistic and Jewish freedom; now they can create their art in freedom.

Dizingoff Centre, Tel Aviv

http://www.presence.co.il/

This is the massive home page of the Dizingoff Centre in Tel Aviv, which displays on its website photos of artwork by numerous Israeli artists. Lots of sculpture, photos, and paintings.

Exhibitions

http://shamash.nysernet.org/nfjc/jets.html

While primarily a resource for museum curators and decision-makers, this site offers the inquiring Web traveler a behind-the-scenes look at how museum exhibitions happen. It lists exhibits currently available for traveling and includes contact information, space requirements, insurance costs, and so on.

Israel Museum, Jerusalem
RECOMMENDED

http://www.imj.org.il/

This cybertour of the Israel Museum in Jerusalem provides a thoughtful presentation of exhibits from each part of its collection, including the Dead Sea Scrolls. You can also find samples of children's art, tour the Art Garden, and get an overview of the entire collection. Art lovers will find photographs of examples from the museum's collection of Judaica, old masters, and contemporary works.

Check out the enlarged version of the Dead Sea Scrolls and see if you can recognize what Jewish ritual object the exhibit resembles.

Israeli Art and Jewelry

http://tucson.com/ajp/

This cyberart gallery coming to you from Englewood, Colorado, offers an interactive catalog of the work of several Jewish and Israeli artists. You'll find pictures of their work, including some very unique and beautiful clothing and religious objects.

Janet Echelman

http://www.fas.harvard.edu/~echelman/

"Making art is like leaving Egypt and going into the wilderness," says Jewish artist and Harvard University artist-in-residence Janet Echelman. See her paintings here.

Maurice Mendjisky

http://orangeraie.azur.fr/mm1_e.htm

Maurice Mendjisky, Polish artist and friend of Picasso and Marc Chagall, drew powerful and moving sketches of the Warsaw Uprising. Meet the artist and view his work at this beautifully designed website.

Mordechai Rosenstein

http://www.netaxs.com/people/zalesjp/

The art of Mordechai Rosenstein—silk screen prints on Jewish themes. Rosenstein also designs synagogue interiors, stained glass, and tapestries. There's also a new line of T-shirts. A very well designed and colorful website and a model for any artist thinking about displaying his or her work online.

Room of Israeli Artists

http://www.art.net/TheGallery/Avi_Room/Israel_Artists.html

A Palo Alto, California, site offers you the work of 11 (at this visit) Israeli artists.

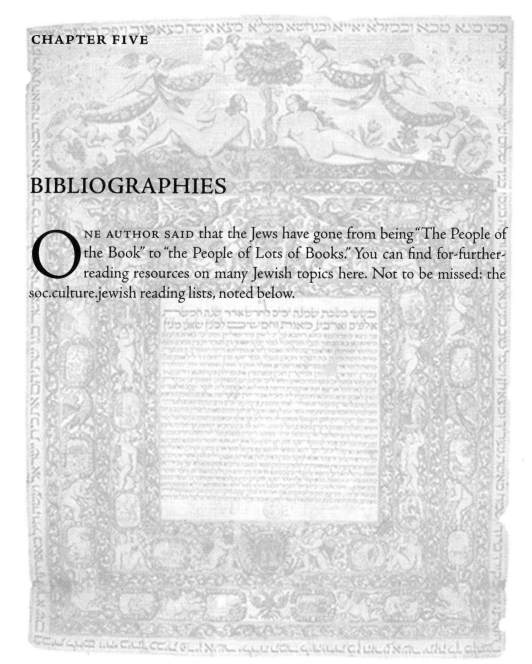

CHAPTER FIVE

BIBLIOGRAPHIES

O NE AUTHOR SAID that the Jews have gone from being "The People of the Book" to "the People of Lots of Books." You can find for-further-reading resources on many Jewish topics here. Not to be missed: the soc.culture.jewish reading lists, noted below.

Feminist-Oriented Prayer

http://world.std.com/~alevin/liturgy.html

A bibliography on prayer books sensitive to feminist concerns, from Jewish Feminist Resources. A typical listing would be the *Kol Haneshama*, the Reconstructionist Siddur; the reviewer praises the work for eliminating masculine references to God in the English but not doing so with the Hebrew. You then find ordering information.

Feminist Theology and Spirituality

http://world.std.com/~alevin/theospirit.html

A bibliography on feminist theology and spirituality, from Jewish Feminist Resources. Only a few of the items are annotated.

Intermarriage

http://www.cis.ohio-state.edu/hypertext/faq/usenet/judaism/reading-lists/intermarriage/

Intermarriage is the subject of this reading list. You'll find topics like "So You're Considering Intermarriage?" "The Traditional Viewpoint," "You've Done the Deed, Coping with Life as an Intermarried" and more.

Jewish History

http://challenge.tiac.net/users/ajhs/ajhbibl.html

Bibliography of essential readings on American Jewish history, from the American Jewish Historical Society. Here you'll find general histories, reference publications, bibliographies and indexes, and periodicals.

32

RECOMMENDED   soc.culture.jewish Reading Lists

http://www.shamash.org/lists/scj-faq/HTML/rl/hl-index.html

An awesome array of Jewish books organized by topic and branch of Judaism. Brought to you by the friendly folks at soc.culture.jewish. See their FAQ (frequently asked questions) as well. An invaluable reference. Organized by topics including traditional liturgy and practice; kabbalah, mysticism, and messianism; Reform; Conservative; Chasidism; Zionism; books for Jewish children; and much more.

Women in Talmud and Jewish Law

http://world.std.com/~alevin/halacha.html

A brief, annotated reading list—books and magazine articles—on women in the Talmud and in Jewish law. The most intriguing title: "Carnal Israel: Reading Sex in Talmud Culture" by Daniel Boyarin.

RECOMMENDED   Women in the Bible

http://world.std.com/~alevin/bible.html

Women in the Bible described; also an excellent reading list. It goes without saying that men get a lot more airtime in the Bible than do women, but a number of women played extremely important roles in biblical times. You may click on the names of Bilhah and Zilpah, Dina, Gomer, Judith, and other biblical-era women and learn about them here.

CHAPTER SIX

CHASIDIC JUDAISM

W HO ARE CHASIDIC JEWS? In 18th-century Eastern Europe, some Jews were attracted to mystics who believed that God could be approached through joy, dance, and song, as well as through intellectual pursuits like Talmud study and traditional prayer. Two centuries later, many Chasidic groups thrive in the United States, in Israel, and across the Jewish world. You can meet a few of these groups on the Internet.

Breslov

http://www.breslov.org/

BRESLOV - JUDAISM WITH HEART

Information Bank on the *TEACHINGS* of outstanding chassidic master
REBBE NACHMAN OF BRESLOV (1772-1810) and ACTIVITIES of the
BRESLOV CHASSIDIC MOVEMENT.

"IF YOU BELIEVE YOU CAN SPOIL,
BELIEVE YOU CAN FIX."

-REBBE NACHMAN OF BRESLOV

"If you believe you can spoil, believe you can fix." So says Rebbe Nachman, a grandson of the Baal Shem Tov and the founder of the Breslov Chasidic movement. Learn all about Breslov Chasidus at their extensive website. You'll find the teachings of Rebbe Nachman, including this comment on boldness: When the sages said "Be bold as a leopard," they were talking about a "kind of forcefulness which is essential for anyone who wants to come closer to God. It is impossible to draw closer to the Tzaddikim and sanctify oneself without it. It entails a certain firmness, determination, and initiative." You'll also find at this website "the latest news in the world of Breslov spirituality"; books and tapes; worldwide resources including classes, tapes, and counseling; and questions and answers about Breslov Chasidus.

RECOMMENDED

Chabad Lubavitch

http://www.chabad.org/

Everything about Chabad, the branch of Chasidic Judaism best known for the late Lubavitcher Rebbe and his commitment to "in-reach," or bringing traditional Judaism to non-Orthodox Jews. A massive website. It features 18 different categories, including Modern Technology and Judaism; The Jewish Woman; The Chabad Philosophy; Worldwide Chabad Directory Listings; Judaism Looks at the World; Send Your Questions on Judaism Here; and Request for a Prayer or a Blessing. I clicked on the "Request for a Blessing" and found an essay on the value of praying at the tombs of the righteous; you also get directions to the burial place of the late Lubavitcher Rebbe in New York City. For those unable to get to New York, a form offers the opportunity to write a prayer request that a Lubavitch individual will take to the gravesite, a touching blend of tradition and technology.

Chabad of Marin County, California

http://linex.com/~yrice/

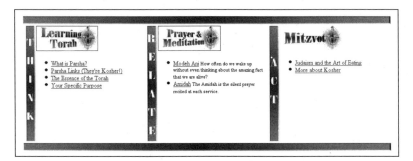

Chabad of Marin presents a website that is simultaneously *very* Chabad and *very* Marin. A New Age approach to traditional Judaism. Meditative, thoughtful, hip. For the nineties-style seeker. The cybervisitor gets three main options: Think, Relate, and Act. Click on "Your Specific Purpose," for example, and read a metaphysical essay on why we're here, presented with stylish text and graphics. Try "Judaism and the Art of Eating" and you'll find a reader-friendly explanation of kashrut replete with thoughtful comments like, "Now, don't get discouraged." Did your *bubbe* and *zaide* tell you about the "spiritual energy" in food? No? That's because they didn't come from Marin. You'll have fun.

Chasidism Reading List (soc.culture.jewish Reading List)

http://www.shamash.org/lists/scj-faq/HTML/rl/joc-index.html

Click on historical Chasidism, Lubavitch, Satmar, Breslov, or other approaches and find extremely useful annotated readings. This is part of the massive and extraordinary soc.culture. jewish resource from Shamash.

CHAPTER SEVEN

CHAT ROOMS, MAILING LISTS, AND NEWSGROUPS

HERE YOU WILL FIND chat rooms, mailing lists, and newsgroups on every topic under the Jewish sun—from Farrakhan, to intermarriage, to personals. Not all of the discussion is useful, intelligent, or even interesting, but, as they say, for those who like this sort of thing, this is the thing they will like.

For help on visiting chat rooms, joining mailing lists, or reading newsgroups, I suggest you purchase a copy of *Dr. Bob's Painless Guide to the Internet* by Bob Rankin (No Starch Press, $12.95 plus shipping, 1-800-420-7240 to order).

Chat Rooms

ENTER THESE CHAT ROOMS and you'll discover discussions ranging from Israeli elections to Jewish singles. Since these chats are all based on the World Wide Web, all you need to do to join and participate is to dial in to the appropriate site and follow the directions there. All the sites have some sort of help if you get stuck. Give 'em a try.

Agmon

http://www.agmon.co.il:8000/

Chat rooms from Agmon, an Israeli service provider, offering no holds barred, anonymous chat. Topics change frequently, but you can usually find a chat room dedicated to Israeli political issues as well as the requisite singles chat.

Sabra Music Center

http://SABRAnet.com/

The Sabra Music Center, "where Israel comes alive on the Internet," offers excerpts of Israeli pop songs from the 70s, 80s, and 90s and a chat room where you can discuss Israeli music.

Webchat Broadcasting System: Israel Chat

http://www.irsociety.com/wbs/visit.html

This is a central source of chat rooms, including chat about Israel. Register on their home page and you'll be able to participate in hundreds of chat rooms.

Mailing Lists

A MAILING LIST, in Internet parlance, offers you the chance to join with like-minded folks in an ongoing discussion of a particular topic of interest to you. You can usually join a mailing list by e-mailing the individual (or automated mailing list server) who maintains the list and simply saying, "subscribe me" (generally "subscribe" if you send mail to a list server). Automatically, you will receive at your e-mail address all the correspondence on that topic from each member of the group. You can make contributions of your own, and all the group members will automatically receive copies of what you have to say.

The downside of mailing lists is that if you subscribe to too many, or if you don't check your e-mail for even a short period of time, you could find yourself swamped with messages. So try one out before you subscribe to a bunch. You can usually quit a mailing list by e-mailing an "unsubscribe me" (or usually "unsubscribe") message to the person (or list server) in charge.

You cannot possibly imagine how many mailing lists already exist on the Internet. Even Carl Sagan cannot count that high. And if you don't like what's out there, you're always free to start your own.

380 Jewish E-Mail Lists

http://acmex.gatech.edu:1995/aviva/jewish-lists.html

Incredible. You'll find 380 Jewish e-mail lists, including instructions on how to sign up for them, at this site. It's hard to know how to describe such a massive number of mailing lists, but you'll find discussions ranging from the Jewish year and Rabbi A. I. Kook, to Torah and Hillel. And, of course, much, much more.

Jewishnet

http://www.mofet.macam98.ac.il/~dovw/jw/l/mail4.html#ZZ

Over 100 Jewish and Israel-related mailing lists, A to Z, courtesy of Jewishnet, the Global Jewish Information Network. Clear, concise, well organized. You'll find topics like a discussion among children and grandchildren of the Holocaust; Ben Gurion University general discussion forum; Golan Heights; Junk (Jewish University Network—I'm not making this stuff up); Proverbs; and Ravnet— the Rabbinical Assembly Discussion Group.

Jewishnet: Jewish and Israeli Interest Mailing Lists

http://jewishnet.net/lis.html

If you thought 380 mailing lists was a lot, check out this site. I couldn't even begin to tell you how many lists you'll find here, but the range is phenomenal. From Holocaust, to hate, to science, aliyah, and Zionism. The links that you'll find at this site will step you through signing up for the mailing lists that interest you. This is the mother lode of Jewish mailing lists.

Science and Business

http://www.tile.net/tile/listserv/israel.html

Mailing lists about Israel with a science and business bent. A lot of the mailing list names make sense only to people who would join them, so if the idea of AMATH-IL, BGU-WEB, LINUX-IL, or TIKSUVON gets you all hot and bothered, you've come to the right place.

Virtual Jerusalem

http://www.virtual.co.il/city_services/lists/

This Israeli commercial site offers 80 to 100 mailing lists on Jewish and Israeli topics. Subjects include Bible commentary, politics, immigration, Jewish music, Jewish humor, medical issues in Israel, Jewish activism, computer jobs in Israel, yada yada yada. Of course, "yada yada yada" is a technical term; it means "and much more." Anyway, the kind folks at Virtual Jerusalem make it extremely easy for you to subscribe to any of their myriad lists.

Newsgroups

NEWSGROUPS OFFER ALL the information of a mailing list without the threat of an overloaded e-mail box. You don't have to join a newsgroup; you just have to find it, and that's where we come in. A newsgroup focuses on one broad topic, say, "fine wine"; you visit the newsgroup and you can read all the comments people have made on the subject and on the comments of the other participants. Most newsgroups organize themselves around "threads," which are smaller topics related to the main one. For example, in the fine wine newsgroup you might have threads discussing vintages, Beaujolais Nouveau, Champagne, and Alcoholics Anonymous.

Remember that there's virtually no editing for content on the Internet, so not everything you read in a newsgroup sounds like it came from a Rhodes scholar. In fact, after 20 minutes of browsing through newsgroups, you'll swear they let the Unabomber have a laptop computer. But try a few out; you never know.

You might want to "lurk"—hang out in the background and read what people are writing—before you jump into the conversation. Also, a lot of people can be very rude to newcomers; the practice is called "flaming." To avoid this rudeness, read a lot to get the hang of the particular newsgroup before you weigh in.

Subscribing to newsgroups is easy with a service like America Online or software like Netcom's Netcruiser; otherwise contact your service provider for information on how to get started.

Genealogy

news:soc.genealogy.jewish

Interesting postings about Jewish genealogy. For example, a writer in France seeks information on a Jewish Los Angeles resident who passed away in 1961; others seek town locations in Poland; others want to know about WWI casualties. A step up from the usual newsgroup blather.

Holocaust Discussion

news:soc.culture.jewish.holocaust

Auschwitz survivors, Holocaust survivors, death camp train timetables, and research papers draw comment here.

Israeli/Middle Eastern Politics

news:talk.politics.mideast

The topics are important public issues, but when I visited, the discussion was somewhat less than edifying. That's the problem with a lot of these unmoderated sites: a lot of blather and not a lot of useful information, opinion, or commentary. Or, to be charitable, maybe I just caught this newsgroup on a bad day.

Israeli-Oriented Newsgroups

news:israel.*

You'll find tons of newsgroups and chat rooms related to Israel here. Weigh in on the latest political or cultural issues.

Music

news:alt.music.jewish

You can discuss all kinds of Jewish music here. When you're done, check out the Music chapter for more music-related resources.

Personals

news:alt.personals.jewish

A contributor describing himself as "young, good-looking, rich, and a doctor" described his trials and travails avoiding women who "scheme and suck up" to him; cybernauts clucked and offered little sympathy. The usual poor taste, witlessness, and pointlessness that mark so much of the newsgroup world. Get a life, not a modem. Harrumph. You'll also find scintillating topics like "What do Jewish women (and men) want?" "We need more women in cyberspace!!!" "Is the Passover seder a time to be with one's family or at the local temple's singles' seder?" Yawn.

Potpourri

news:soc.culture.jewish

Farrakhan, intermarriage, and Alicia Silverstone attracted comment when I visited.

Shamash Newsgroups

http://www.racersworld.com/~rickh/shamash3.html

More than 100 newsgroups on every conceivable Jewish subject are linked to this website. You can't imagine the variety; see for yourself.

Society and Culture

news:soc.culture.israel

The peace process, terrorism, and Farrakhan dominate the conversation here.

World War II

news:soc.history.war.world-war-ii

This World War II–focused newsgroup discusses topics such as Zyklon B—how dangerous?; bombing of concentration camps; and who contributed most to the defeat of Nazi Germany?

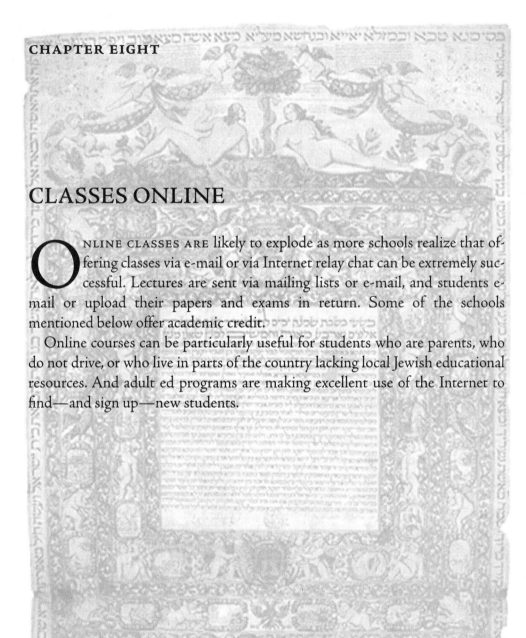

CHAPTER EIGHT

CLASSES ONLINE

O NLINE CLASSES ARE likely to explode as more schools realize that offering classes via e-mail or via Internet relay chat can be extremely successful. Lectures are sent via mailing lists or e-mail, and students e-mail or upload their papers and exams in return. Some of the schools mentioned below offer academic credit.

Online courses can be particularly useful for students who are parents, who do not drive, or who live in parts of the country lacking local Jewish educational resources. And adult ed programs are making excellent use of the Internet to find—and sign up—new students.

The Holocaust

http://www.umassd.edu/cybered/theholocaust.html

Register here for an online, full-semester, apparently noncredit course on the Holocaust from the University of Massachusetts Dartmouth campus. An intriguing use of the Internet. You'll find a detailed syllabus, assignments, and even a take-home final exam. UMass/Dartmouth offers credit and noncredit courses online.

The Holocaust in Historical Context

http://www.dsu.nodak.edu/course/artscience/socbehav/holocau.html

Study "The Holocaust in Historical Context" with Dickinson State University in North Dakota in this online extension course. You study via e-mail, and there are assignments and papers that you can submit via e-mail or U.S. mail. Interestingly, a lot of the "recommended readings" are links to Jewish-related websites, most of which are reviewed in this book. Anyone interested in offering courses online ought to visit this site to see how to do it.

Milah

http://www.jer1.co.il/edu/milah/

Milah, a Jerusalem ulpan or Hebrew school for immigrants and others, says that it is about to offer online modern Hebrew classes through this webpage. On our most recent visit, there was no target date for the classes, but by the time you read this it might be in business online. Give it a shot.

RECOMMENDED   ORT Educational Resources

http://www.ort.org/edu/edu.htm

Great educational and related links for kids and schools. Includes
links for teachers, kids, question services, educational conferences, schools online, games, festivals, and more. For example, Question Services offers e-mail addresses for Scientist-on-Tap, run by the
Jet Propulsion Laboratory, supporting the Galileo and Hubble tele-
scopes; Ask Dr. Math, run by Swarthmore College's Geometry
Forum; and Wordsmith, which looks up dictionary definitions and
thesaurus entries and unscrambles acronyms and anagrams. A wonderful and imaginatively chosen set of resources for educators or anyone interested in learning more about Judaism.

RECOMMENDED   Project Genesis

http://www.torah.org/

"Torah on the Information Superhighway" is how this group
describes itself. Free online classes, taught by means of
weekly free lectures delivered to your e-mail address. The teachers are
prominent rabbis and the "classes" cover every topic imaginable that
relates to traditional Judaism. Subjects include Jewish philosophy,
liturgy, ethics, and law. The approach is Orthodox, but the Project
Genesis people take care to discuss matters in ways that non-Orthodox Jews can appreciate. Well worth a visit.

CHAPTER NINE

COLLEGES, UNIVERSITIES, AND OTHER RESOURCES FOR STUDENTS

T HIS CHAPTER FEATURES home pages, websites, and more from a wide variety of institutions of higher learning in the United States and Israel, plus further resources for students. The best marketing move in history may have been providing free e-mail and Internet access to college students. For students and recent graduates, voyaging through cyberspace is as natural as picking up the phone and calling one's folks, collect, and asking for money. Seriously, if you've been getting and sending e-mail since freshman year, and surfing the Internet since high school, you're an excellent candidate for an Internet access account of your own after you leave school. Which explains why so many colleges and universities have websites, links, and connections, many of which take you to Jewish organizations.

The downside, right now, is that a lot of schools aren't making much of their Internet connection. Few schools have really smashing, attractive, or informative websites. It's not like the Archeology or Art sites, for example, where you can just noodle around and find cool stuff. A lot of the sites in this section, alas, are fairly prosaic. But if you're trying to get information about a specific school, department of Jewish studies, or Jewish campus organization, you're highly likely to find what you need here without wasting time online.

In the United States

Albert Einstein College of Medicine

http://www.aecom.yu.edu/

What's up, doc? Find out here, at the home page of Yeshiva University's medical school located in New York City. Also includes weblinks to other scientific and medical resources, including the various medical departments at Einstein and related facilities like Long Island Jewish Medical Center and Yeshiva University's home page.

Columbia University

http://www.columbia.edu/cu/jsu/

All things Jewish at Columbia. An exceptionally sophisticated and well-designed website, offering links to all the various Jewish groups on campus. You can find out about prayer services for all branches of Judaism, Jewish studies, food, holidays, and lists of synagogues throughout New York City.

Cornell University

http://www.cornell.edu/Academic/Courses95/AS88.17.html

A brief description of the Jewish Studies program at Cornell, and not much else at our last visit.

Hebrew College

http://www.shamash.org/hc/

Hebrew College, located in Brookline, Massachusetts, serves a community of 2,000 students and participants with undergraduate and graduate degree programs, education training programs, high school programs, Jewish music programs, and much more. Cross-registration is possible at a wide range of Boston area universities and schools.

Hebrew Union College

http://cwis.usc.edu/dept/huc-la/

The facts about Hebrew Union College in Los Angeles, the West Coast educational arm of the Reform movement.

Princeton University

http://www.princeton.edu/~pressman/jewish.html#princeton

Jewish resources at Princeton University, including links to libraries and the Princeton Hillel. Also offers a tour of the Center for Jewish Life at Princeton, providing answers to frequently asked questions.

University of Pennsylvania

http://futures.wharton.upenn.edu/~putter71/roots.html

University of Pennsylvania students can learn about their heritage at this website, home of Roots, dedicated to the pursuit of Jewish knowledge. Roots is a weekly event at the Penn Hillel; Jewish students pair off and study Judaism in what the website calls a "bubbling center of excitement." You can "virtually do Roots"—sign up and get a net-partner for your Judaic studies.

In Israel

Bar-Ilan University

http://www.biu.ac.il:80/BIU/

Israel's third largest university, Bar Ilan, bridges the gap between the secular and observant communities. The website has plenty of room to grow.

Hebrew University

http://www1.huji.ac.il/

The home page of the Hebrew University of Jerusalem. Learn about the campus. You can also connect, from your own computer, to libraries and databases in Hebrew and English in and out of Israel. Accessing these libraries can make your research chores a lot easier.

Melton Centre for Jewish Education in the Diaspora

http://www2.huji.ac.il/www_melton/top.html

The Melton Centre for Jewish Education in the Diaspora, at Hebrew University, offers graduate programs in Jewish education. You'll find course offerings, details about minicourses, the Centre's goals, and, under the category of "Something for Everyone—Just Plain Folks," the promise of information for nonspecialists. The Pedagogic Resource Centre and Library for Jewish Education can be accessed by Telnet.

Open University of Israel

http://www.openu.ac.il/

The Open University of Israel offers home study programs leading to undergraduate degrees. In existence since 1974, its students include soldiers, the homebound, those in distant corners of Israel, the ultra-Orthodox, and others. Learn about their offerings here at this attractive website.

Tel Aviv University

http://www.tau.ac.il/

Tel Aviv University's home page. Information about various faculty and departments as well as links to related home pages.

Weizmann Institute

http://www.weizmann.ac.il/

Science types will appreciate the home page of the Weizmann Institute of Science in Israel. The rest of us can marvel at the long words. There's very little here for the nonscientist, which is really a pity—the displays they could put on for the rest of us could be dazzling. A word to the wise.

Other Resources for Students

Association of Jewish Sixth Formers

http://www.ort.org/anjy/orgtions/aj6/aj6.htm

A new group for Jewish students in the U.K. Of interest strictly to Brits; not a lot for us Yanks here at this time.

China Judaic Studies Association

http://www.oakton.edu/~friend/chinajews.html

Judaic Studies in China is the topic of this Illinois-based webpage. University courses, tours to China, awards, and publications. You can also find some short essays, with such topics as "A Brief Introduction to Kaifeng," and the preface to a book called *The Jews of Shanghai* by Pan Guang.

Educational Programs in Israel

gopher://israel.nysernet.org:70/11/

This gopher menu lists educational programs in Israel.

Jerusalem Fellowships

http://www.urich.edu/~provost/Resources/

Who would have thought that hidden away in listings for the University of Richmond you can find information about the Jerusalem Fellowships for Study in Israel and month-long summer programs to bring North American Jews to Israel and prepare them for leadership roles? And better still, if you live in the New York area, UJA Federation and New York Hillel might even pick up your airfare. Is this a great country or what? No photos, but some excellent information.

Kesher

http://www.netspace.org/~mharvey/kesher/#WhatIs

College students can connect with Kesher, a nationwide organization for Reform Judaism on campus. With contact names, e-mail links, information about the organization and its services, and ways for you to get involved.

"Official Unofficial List"   RECOMMENDED

http://www1.snunit.k12.il/snunit_e/isschool.htm

"The 1996 Official Unofficial List of Israeli Schools on the Internet" is an excellent resource if you're thinking about going to school in Israel. E-mail and home page links make a long list of Israeli schools instantly accessible for you. Begin your search here.

Seminary of Judaic Studies

http://149.105.1.3/israel/bm/index.html

The Jewish Theological Seminary's branch in Israel, the Seminary of Judaic Studies, also known as the Bet Midrash, offers programs including rabbinic and educational studies, a year in Israel study program, and an M.A. in Jewish Studies. A brief website, with text only.

CHAPTER TEN

CONSERVATIVE JUDAISM

WHEN YOU CONSIDER the size of Conservative Judaism in the United States, it seems likely that its representation on the World Wide Web will increase and multiply. Here are some of the most important and useful sites related to Conservative Judaism that can be found on the Internet.

Jewish Theological Seminary

RECOMMENDED

http://www.jtsa.edu/

The Jewish Theological Seminary, or JTS, in New York City is the spiritual and intellectual home of Conservative Judaism. JTS offers undergraduate, graduate, and rabbinical training in what it describes as North America's most extensive program of advanced Jewish studies. Its website is excellent—a vast, comprehensive, and extremely well-organized guide to JTS. You'll also find current and back issues of *Masoret Magazine* (*masoret* has many meanings, including Jewish tradition, legacy, and heritage); commentaries on the weekly Torah portion; news; and JTS history—in short, a treasure trove of information about Conservative Judaism.

Koach

http://uscj.org/koach/

The Hebrew word for "strength." Lots of programming for Conservative Jewish college students as well as interesting resources including an e-mail list server, archives, an events calendar, and *D'vrei Torah*. Of special note is the KOACH Campus Creative Grants Program, which enables college students to find money to sponsor programs, projects, and events.

Masoret Magazine

http://www.jtsa.edu/masoret/

Masoret Magazine is the publication of the Jewish Theological Seminary. You'll find the entire magazine online at this site. Recent articles include "Will the Real Crisis Please Stand Up?" in which Rabbi David Wolpe examines the ever-growing list of issues facing our community, and "Finding Her Way," written by newly ordained Ben Wyler about her experiences as the first woman rabbi in Germany.

Temple Etz Chaim, Sherman Oaks, California   RECOMMENDED

http://www.rain.org/~etzchaim/index.html#index

Meet the 600-family congregation of Temple Etz Chaim in Sherman Oaks, California. This extensive and thorough website could serve as a model for temples and synagogues designing their own webpages. You'll find messages from the rabbi and cantor; descriptions of programs; a statement of purpose; even information on the men's club and bingo. What a great way to unite the congregation.

Temple Shalom of Newton, Massachusetts

http://www.Ultranet.com/~shalom

The attractive web page for this Newton, Massachusetts, congregation features sermons and articles by the rabbis, calendars and schedules, programs, activities, and more.

United Synagogue of Conservative Judaism   RECOMMENDED

http://www.uscj.org

The United Synagogue of
Conservative Judaism

Welcome to the USCJ's Home Page on the World Wide Web!

This site represents the synagogue arm of Conservative Judaism with a wealth of information on Conservative Judaism, including e-mail and gopher resources, and connections to dozens of Conservative synagogue groups. Excerpts from *Review Magazine* and position papers on current issues such as the religious equality amendments now in Congress.

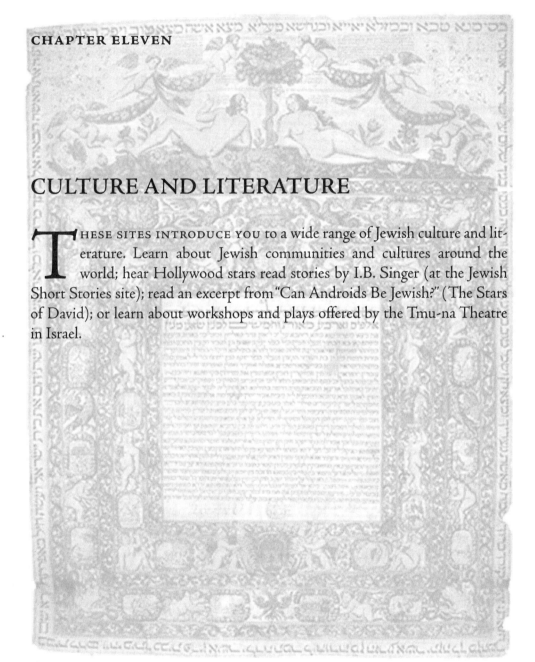

CHAPTER ELEVEN

CULTURE AND LITERATURE

THESE SITES INTRODUCE YOU to a wide range of Jewish culture and literature. Learn about Jewish communities and cultures around the world; hear Hollywood stars read stories by I.B. Singer (at the Jewish Short Stories site); read an excerpt from "Can Androids Be Jewish?" (The Stars of David); or learn about workshops and plays offered by the Tmu-na Theatre in Israel.

92nd Street Y, New York City

http://www.92ndsty.org/

If you can't find it at the 92nd Street Y, you can't find it. The 92nd Street Y is one of the leading cultural institutions in the United States, and a good reason to move to New York, offering concert and dance performances, lectures and literary readings, Jewish lectures and celebrations, and who knows what all else. A gorgeous webpage, with mostly listings of upcoming events.

Ahad Ha-am

http://www.hypertext.com/atheisms/ahadhaa.html

A brief biography of Ahad Ha-am, one of the leading figures in Zionist literature, at this site dedicated to atheism. You'll also find essays by or about Sherwin Wine, Martin Buber, Mordecai Kaplan, and atheistic traditions in other cultures.

Jewish Folklore in Israel

http://www.tau.ac.il/%7Egila1/folklore/

Spectacular. Well-written essays, tons of information, links to many cultural institutions in Israel. Learn about Jewish communities of the Arab countries, Eastern Europe, the former Soviet Union, Central and Western Europe, South and North America, and Africa.

RECOMMENDED   ## Jewish Short Stories

http://www.kcrw.org/b/jss.html

J ewish short stories from Eastern Europe and beyond. Top Hollywood stars read stories by I. B. Singer, Sholem Aleichem, Grace
Paley, and others. Let your computer tell you a Jewish bedtime story.

Michael Elkin's Jewish Entertainment Home Page

http://www.netaxs.com/%7Eelkin/

M ichael Elkin writes columns about Jews in all fields of entertainment—TV, movies, theater, and music—for Phila-
delphia's *Jewish Exponent*. You can find his columns archived here. Recent topics: Paulette Goddard; the Jewish codirector of *Pocahontas*;
Carl Reiner; *The American President*; Heidi Fleiss.

National Federation for Jewish Culture

gopher://shamash.nysernet.org/hh/nfjc/

Jewish museums, theaters, and all else related to Jewish culture. You'll find it here. Links to dozens of Jewish museums and cultural groups across the U.S., doctoral programs, theater news—it's all here. Exhibitions I found when I visited were "The Holocaust Project: From Darkness into light, by Judy Chicago"; "Stalin's Forgotten Israel: Birobidzhan and the Making of a Soviet Jewish Homeland"; and "Too Jewish?: Claiming Jewish Identity in the Age of Muliculturalism."

The Stars of David

http://www.the-stars-of-david.com/cover.html

This is a sales pitch for *The Stars of David*, a two-volume compendium of Jewish science fiction. You'll find excerpts and ordering information. Sample 200-page stories: "Can Androids Be Jewish?" and "Miriam's World." Appropriate for advanced seventh and eighth graders through adults.

Tmu-na Theatre, Israel

http://www.pf1.co.il/tmu-na/

Tmu-Na Theatre, located in Tel Aviv, offers workshops and plays; get to know the company and its offerings here. Theater and show schedules; a 25% discount for tickets ordered online. Play titles in their 15 year history include *Transit Hotel*, *Dress*, and *Real Time*. Many of their works have been produced at the Edinburgh and Glasgow Arts Festivals.

CHAPTER TWELVE

DANCE

UNTIL THE INTERNET came along, the only way to learn Israeli dancing was to show up at a beginners' group, learn the steps (sort of) to one dance, and then hang around feeling out of it for the rest of the evening until the dance that you learned came up. Meanwhile, everyone else is leaping around and knowing all the steps while you're sitting there saying to yourself, "For this I missed Seinfeld."

Not anymore. You can actually learn to dance with your computer. (No, that didn't come out right. You can't actually dance physically with your computer unless it's a laptop, and if you do that, you'd better keep the shades drawn.) Your computer can teach you to dance, and the good news is that it won't keep trying to lead. You can visit dance sites on the Web that actually provide the foot patterns for more Israeli dances than you ever knew existed. You can also learn where to dance, in the U.S. and in Israel.

There's nothing like privacy to give you the freedom to try something new. Even if you have two left feet you should check these sites out. They're a remarkable use of the Internet.

Find Out About Dance

ftp://ftp.bellcore.com/pub/ernie/israeli/homepage.html

The links at this FTP site allow you to search for information about Israeli dances, composers, and the like. Search for dance classes in the U.S., even read back issues of the *Video-in-Motion* newsletter, with updates on the latest Israel dances and the company's series of commercially available dance videos.

Israeli Folk Dances   RECOMMENDED

http://www.artsci.wustl.edu/~jclerman/folkdance/dances.html

Click on the Israeli circle or line dance of your choice and through the magic of Telnet the steps appear right on your computer screen.

Salsa

http://www.inch.com/~judyf/salsa/telaviv.htm

Salsa lovers can merengue to their corazons' content at LatinGate. You'll find listings of where to dance, how to dance, where to listen to music, and more. Salsa, merengue, lambada, cubia. Dance classes at Tel Aviv clubs.

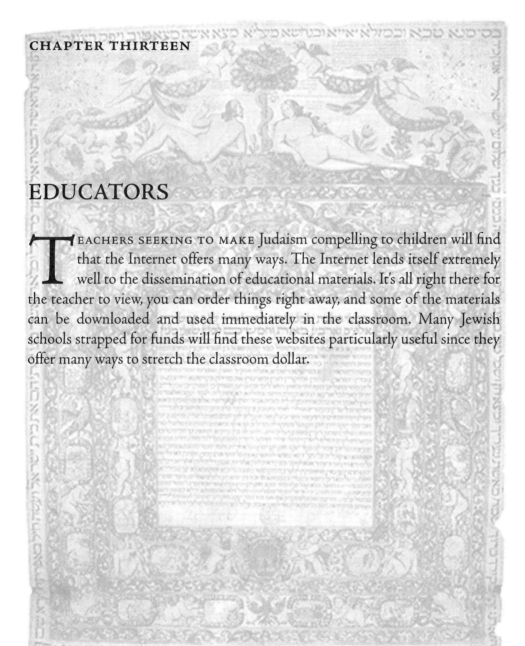

CHAPTER THIRTEEN

EDUCATORS

TEACHERS SEEKING TO MAKE Judaism compelling to children will find that the Internet offers many ways. The Internet lends itself extremely well to the dissemination of educational materials. It's all right there for the teacher to view, you can order things right away, and some of the materials can be downloaded and used immediately in the classroom. Many Jewish schools strapped for funds will find these websites particularly useful since they offer many ways to stretch the classroom dollar.

Agency for Jewish Education

http://shamash.nysernet.org/ejin/brijnet/ed/orgs/aje/aje.html

The Agency for Jewish Education, based in London, offers teacher training, curriculum planning, and other services for educators. They produce the Lamdeni reading series, which uses books, audio- and videotapes, and other media.

BJE Resources   RECOMMENDED

http://www.slip.net/~bjesf/resources.winter95.html

The attractive, useful, and user-friendly home page of the Bureau of Jewish Education of the San Francisco area. Teach or learn about Jerusalem with their movies and other educational resources. Titles include *Jerusalem: The Soul of a People*; and *Shalom Sesame*, the Israeli coproduction of *Sesame Street*. The focus is Jerusalem 3000.

Community Foundation for Jewish Education

http://www.mcs.net/~cfje/home.html

The Community Foundation for Jewish Education provides educational resources for educators in the Reconstructionist, Reform, and Conservative movements in such areas as early childhood, adult education, and professional development. Get to know them here.

Conpu-Torah Learning Corporation

http://home.aol.com/ctlc

Compu-Torah Learning Corporation offers consulting for schools seeking to establish Jewish education via computer.

Hadracha Resource Database

http://www.ort.org/anjy/hadracha/had_home.htm

Course materials for teachers in Orthodox education at this site include such resources as Jerusalem 3000, a biography of Rav Kook, and a collection of essays about Yitzhak Rabin. Sponsored by A Network of Jewish Youth.

Holocaust Studies

http://www.socialstudies.com/holo.html

You'll find resources on Holocaust studies for teachers at this site sponsored by Social Studies School Service. You can search for and order books, videos, and photos. Subjects include "Hitler and Nazism," "Resistance," "Righteous Ones," "Children and Teens," "Moral Issues," and "Prejudice."

Israel Educational Television

http://www.ventura.co.il/e/edutv/start.htm

Teachers can order videocassettes of Israel Educational Television programming for young people at this website.

Jerusalem Through the Windows of Time

http://www.youth.org.il/jer.htm

Jerusalem Through the Windows of Time offers educators ways to bring the story of Jerusalem to children. From the Joint Authority for Jewish Zionist Education.

Kidlink

http://www.KIDLINK.ORG/KIDLEADER-HEBREW/listmail.html

Educators can make use of the Kidlink, a mailing list dedicated to Jewish education with a focus on Israel.

Lamda Community

http://www.lamda.org.il/f/plamda.html

Created by the Tel-Aviv University Science and Technology Information Center, the Lamda Community is for educators interested in elementary science education. An online community, with discussion groups, curricula, a newsletter, and a "science response team," providing science background on news events. You'll find recources like a Thinking Toolkit, a "collection of pedagogic tools for the science teacher," and a Discussorium, which is a newsgroup-like means of conversing about science. This is a rapidly growing site.

Missing in Action

gopher://gopher.jer1.co.il:70/11/ped/epa/eng/mia

Israeli soldiers missing in action and the Jewish responsibility to redeem them is the topic of this gopher menu. Aimed at Israeli high school students, a netcruiser can learn a lot about the way Israel educates—and looks after—her own.

RECOMMENDED

ORT Educational Resources

http://www.ort.org/edu/edu.htm

Great educational and related links for kids and schools. Includes links for teachers, kids, question services, educational conferences, schools online, games, festivals, and more. A wonderful resource for educators or anyone interested in learning more about Judaism. You'll find, for example, "Navigating the Bible," which teaches kids—or older people rediscovering their Jewish roots—about their Bar or Bat Mitzvah portion, and "Jerusalem Game," an interactive learning game about the sites of Jerusalem.

Pedagogic Center

http://www.jajz-ed.org.il/

Teachers and others in the Jewish education community will find invaluable the resources at the Pedagogic Center in Israel. How to teach everything relating to Judaism, all in one website.

Reach & Teach

http://pages.prodigy.com/AZ/kinder/Holocausteducation.html

A free resource for Holocaust education, for the benefit of teachers, educators, schools, colleges, and organizations. The Reach & Teach Group consists of several Holocaust survivors, their offspring, and educators located in various parts of the country.

Their primary aim is to reach out to individuals, particularly the younger generation, and to teach, educate, and inform them about the Holocaust, the Kindertransport, and related World War II historical facts. Education is by computer and personal visits. Topics include everything from prewar German economic and social conditions through the end of the war—and beyond.

Vancouver Holocaust Centre

http://hoshi.cic.sfu.ca/~spec-state/vhec.html

The basics about the Vancouver Holocaust Centre, which acts as a resource for teachers and students learning about the Holocaust.

74

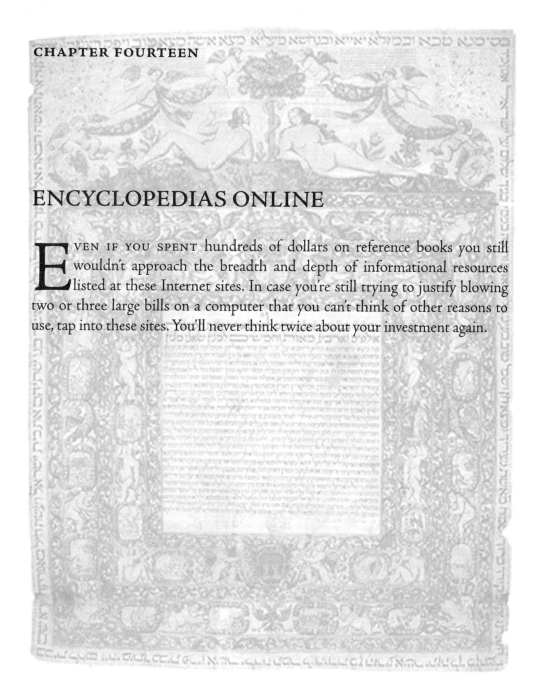

ENCYCLOPEDIAS ONLINE

EVEN IF YOU SPENT hundreds of dollars on reference books you still wouldn't approach the breadth and depth of informational resources listed at these Internet sites. In case you're still trying to justify blowing two or three large bills on a computer that you can't think of other reasons to use, tap into these sites. You'll never think twice about your investment again.

Anti-Semitism

gopher://gopher.jer1.co.il:70/11/fight

Opposing hate crimes, fascism, and dissemination of the "Protocols of Zion" are the subjects of this gopher menu. You'll find resources like "Modern Neo-Fascist, Nazi Groups," "New Jersey Commission on Holocaust Education," "Holocaust and Holocaust Denial Archives," and "The Holocaust: A Guide for Pennsylvania Teachers." Download the index first since there's a lot of information at this site—much of it fascinating.

Basics of Judaism

http://www.cs.ruu.nl/wais/html/na-dir/judaism/FAQ/11-Miscellaneous.html

Witty and informative, this FAQ file answers the questions often asked by those interested in knowing more about Judaism.

For example, the authors explain that the derogatory term "kike" originates with the Yiddish word "keikl," meaning "circle." Some Jewish immigrants at Ellis Island could not sign their own names and instead signed with a circle instead of a cross; thus the term came to refer, rudely, to Jews.

Classic Jewish Texts Seminar

http://www.ncc.com/dvjcc/ClassicTextSem.html#INTRODUCTION

This extremely interesting way to learn about Jewish texts comes to you from the home page of the Dallas Jewish community. You'll learn how to set up a study group in your community so that you and your friends can examine classic Jewish texts for yourselves. The Internet at its best.

Documents of Jewish Belief

http://www.netaxs.com/~expweb/jewish_belief.html

A website with monster potential. Actual texts of documents, encyclopedia entries, museum exhibits, and the like for all the branches of Judaism. There were just a few things at my last visit, like the Tanya, the basic text of Chabad Chasidus; three key documents in the history of Reform Judaism; and a museum exhibition on Jewish author and philosopher Franz Rozensweig. May the people behind this webpage turn it into a vast repository of Jewish learning.

RECOMMENDED

Eliezer Segal

http://www.ucalgary.ca/~elsegal/Shokel/Art_Index.html

Professor Eliezer Segal of the University of Calgary, a Hero of the Jewish Internet, writes excellent, clear, enjoyable articles about the Jewish holidays, Jewish weddings, and everything Jewish that you can think of. Now, unless you subscribe to the *Calgary Jewish Star* or the *Calgary Jewish Free Press*, how would you know about Professor Segal? That's right. You wouldn't. Thank you, Internet. Visit this site and learn tons about Judaism. Also visit his Page of Talmud, Varieties of Orthodox Judaism, and Ten Sefirot of the Kaballah.

RECOMMENDED

Hebrew Text of the Tanach

http://shamash.org/tanach/text.html

Full Hebrew text of the Tanach (Hebrew Bible), Talmud Bavli (Babylonian Talmud), and Talmud Yerushalmi (Jerusalem Talmud) is available from Snunit at the Hebrew University in Jerusalem for Web browsing. Links between Bible verses and the locations in which they are mentioned in the Talmud make this an extraordinary, time-saving resource. These texts, along with Mishne Torah leRambam,

Mishna, and Tosefta, are available for downloading along with DOS browsing software in the MTR package available free from Snunit.

Tanach stands for Torah (Five Books of Moses, Genesis through Deuteronomy), N'vi'im (the Prophets), and C'tuvim (Holy Writings—Psalms, Proverbs, and the rest of the Hebrew Bible). In the unforgettable words of Rabbi Judah haNasi, "This is like totally tubular, dude."

You can also find out how to get your browser to display Hebrew (you need to download and install Hebrew fonts—see the Software section of this book for more information).

It's Academic

gopher://veronica.psi.com:2347/7?Judaism

This address will bring you to a lengthy gopher menu with files relating to Judaism, prayer, the Midrash, first-century Judaism, and dozens of other topics by academics. Many academics make their works available for free here.

Jewish Communications Network   RECOMMENDED

http://www.jcn18.com/

The Jewish Communications Network seeks to create a virtual Jewish community for individuals, families, writers, and all Jews. There's a lot going on here: discussion groups on current Jewish and Israel events; a "newsstand" offering articles on or of interest to Jews; a news service; and entertainment features. For example, the week before Passover the JCN offered an interactive Haggadah. You e-mail in your comments on a part of the Passover story and they're combined with other folks' thoughts to create a new commentary.

Jewish Outreach Institute

http://wwwuser.gc.cuny.edu/cjs/joi.htm

The Jewish Outreach Institute discusses intermarriage in an intelligent and sensitive way. You'll find well-written essays under "Books Online"; an extensive national directory of outreach programs; and support for intermarrying and "interdating" Jews, their significant others, and their families.

RECOMMENDED

Judaism 101

http://members.aol.com/jewfaq/index.htm#Contents

Judaism 101 is an extremely cogent and well-organized guide to traditional Jewish (Orthodox) belief. All about Jewish people, places, symbols, deeds, holidays, and much more. All of your questions will be answered in this online, hypertext-linked "book." And you can download the entire set of information, including graphics, in a file that you can open and read in Microsoft Word!

Maqom

http://www.compassnet.com/~maqom/#mailing

Rabbi Judith Z. Abrams of Houston, Texas, author of five books on the Talmud, has a mission: to bring Talmud study to as many people as possible. To that end she has created the thoughtful and intellectually delightful Maqom website for Talmud study.

A graceful writer and an expert on the Talmud, Rabbi Abrams teaches Talmud at the site and also sets up her students (you, perhaps?) in traditional *chevrusas*, or pairs of students. Study alone or with someone else, but do not miss her fascinating take on the Talmud.

Nysernet Gopher Menu

gopher://israel.nysernet.org/11/lists

Everything about everything is the best way to describe this mas-sive gopher menu from the nice people at Nysernet. The list de-fies organization; jump in and see what you find. A lot has to do with education and campuses, but you'll find all sorts of links to items like Torah and grammar discussions; *Bridges Bridges*, the Jewish feminist journal; "Second Generation," a discussion among children and grandchildren of the Holocaust; "GayJews"; genealogy; *Jewish Week*; The Canadian Council for Reform Judaism Discussion; and much, much more. Surf on in; remember to pack a lunch.

ORT Hebrew Language Series   RECOMMENDED

http://www.ort.org/ort/hebrew/start.htm

Learn Hebrew here with ORT's web-minded interactive language series. Clear and concise lessons that will have you speaking He-brew like a native. This is an interactive series under development for teaching modern Hebrew. The 60 units develop basic reading, listen-ing, and speaking skills in Hebrew. In the later levels, the units involve e-mailing your answers, using IRC (Internet Relay Chat), and play-ing multiuser games in Hebrew. You'll even find free, downloadable, educational games to play to help you to learn Hebrew. And the best part is that it's all free.

Okay. A TV interviewer in Jerusalem asks four Jews, one Israeli, one American, one Russian, and one Pole, "Excuse me, but what is your opinion on the high cost of meat?"

The Pole says, "What is meat?"

The Russian says, "What is opinion?"

The American asks, "What is high cost?"

The Israeli asks, "What is Excuse me?"

ORT's Jewish World

http://www.ort.org/jeworld/jeworld.htm

ORT's Jewish World is a unique search facility that allows you to find all topics of a Jewish nature across the whole of the Internet. A very useful and powerful search tool for beginning your trek.

RECOMMENDED

Soc.Culture.Jewish FAQ

http://www.shamash.org/lists/scj-faq/HTML/

Soc.culture.jewish FAQ and Reading List is probably the single most vital resource on the entire Jewish Internet. Extremely well-written essays on every topic you can think of—every branch of Judaism, every philosophy, every everything is represented here. Breathtaking, encyclopedic, not to be missed. Daniel P. Faigin, the organizer, truly merits his title of Hero of the Jewish Internet.

Tikkun

http://www.panix.com/~tikkun/

Tikkun magazine's home page. Founded by author and educator Michael Lerner, *Tikkun* is an excellent journal of progressive social and religious thought. Lerner is very close to the First Lady, and his "politics of meaning" have had enormous resonance in the Clinton White House. This website offers articles, editorials, and more from the current issue. Articles at a recent visit included "After O.J. and the Farrakhan March," "Is Healing Possible?" and "Jews in Beijing." I also found editorials by Michael Lerner, including one titled "The Oppression of Singles and Sucking Up to the Rich."

University of Minnesota Gopher Menu

gopher://gopher.tc.umn.edu/11/

From the University of Minnesota, the original home of the gopher, comes this gopher menu of sources of information throughout the Middle East. Includes links to most Israeli universities, including the Technion, Ben Gurion, and the Weizmann Institute, as well as Middle East nations including Tunisia, Iran, and Egypt. A vital resource. (Choose "Other Gopher and Information Servers," then "Middle East" to see the list.)

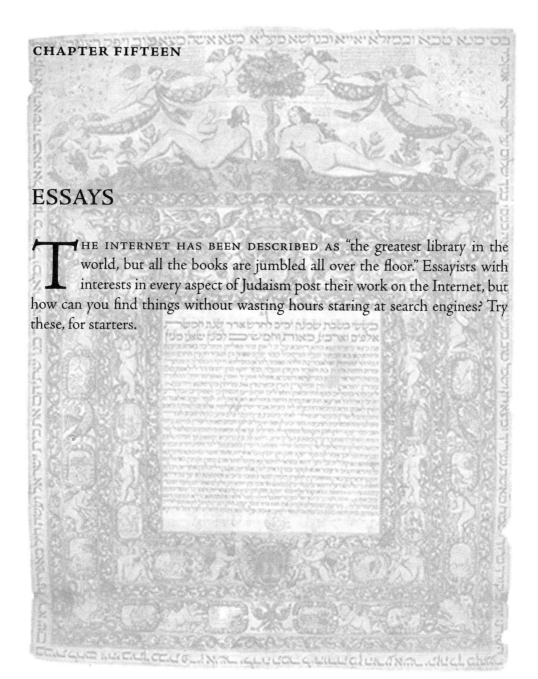

CHAPTER FIFTEEN

ESSAYS

THE INTERNET HAS BEEN DESCRIBED AS "the greatest library in the world, but all the books are jumbled all over the floor." Essayists with interests in every aspect of Judaism post their work on the Internet, but how can you find things without wasting hours staring at search engines? Try these, for starters.

Anti-Proselytizing

http://www.clark.net/pub/mpowers/j4j/web/

This group counters Christian proselytizing of Jews with programming, articles, testimony of Jews converted to Christianity, and an "Ask the Rabbi" section. Includes answers to questions about why Jews do not accept Christian religious beliefs.

Astrology

ftp://ftp.lehigh.edu/pub/listserv/ioudaios-l/Articles/lnastro

It's not exactly Linda Goodman's Sun Signs. This website offers a scholarly look at ancient astrology by Lester J. Ness of Indiana University, from an article originally published in *Archeology in the Biblical World*. As Dick Smothers once said, "I'm an Asparagus. I was born under the sign of 'We Never Close.'"

Gaucher Disease

http://q.continuum.net/~wrosen/gaucher.html

Information about Gaucher disease, which disproportionately affects Jews of Eastern European origin.

Gossip

http://www.torah.org/learning/gossip/

This excerpt from the Project Genesis home page—traditionally minded purveyors of "Torah on the Information Superhighway"—offers a guide to Jewish laws prohibiting gossip. I'll bet you didn't know that Jewish law actually considers matters like gossip, but it does. The Chofetz Chaim, one of the great sages of Jewish history, wrote a guide to "Observing One's Language"; here's a cybercommentary on it from Project Genesis.

Hilary Ostrov, the Internet Traveler

http://haven.uniserve.com/~hostrov/jwb/

Cruise the Jewish Internet with Hilary Ostrov's weekly column in Vancouver's *Jewish Western Bulletin*. Ms. Ostrov asks questions and finds answers at websites across the globe; she recommends sites and offers hypertext links at this Shamash website. Shamash, the Jewish Internet Consortium, is described in Chapter 27 (Lists, Links, and Databases).

Jewish History

http://www.demon.co.uk/solbaram/index.html

Essays on Jewish history.

Jewish Studies Judaic eJournal

http://shamash.nysernet.org/ajs/jsjej.html

Welcome to the

JEWISH STUDIES JUDAICA eJOURNAL

World Wide Web Home Page

The *Jewish Studies Judaica eJournal* (eJournal is not a misprint—it means electronic journal). An important resource for academics, this monthly online publication from Shamash offers articles, news about academia, and job listings that might be hard to find elsewhere.

Jonathan Pollard

http://www.csuohio.edu/tagar/jona.html

Jonathan Pollard is the topic of this website. Pollard, an American, was imprisoned for espionage on behalf of Israel; his supporters believe his punishment has been extremely disproportionate to his crime. Read all about it here.

King Solomon

http://www.demon.co.uk/solbaram/articles/fn2.html

An interesting essay on Israel in the time of King Solomon. Was he really the glorious, wise ruler history claims, or is there more to the story? Manfred Davidmann writes that "oppression increased during Solomon's reign and some of the country had already been lost by the time he died." You be the judge.

Languages

http://www-ala.doc.ic.ac.uk/~rap/Ethnologue/eth.cgi/Israel/

Ever wonder how many Israelis speak Amharic, the language of Ethiopian Jews? If you check this Ethnologue database, you'll discover that the number is 50,000 to 60,000 and that they've been printing the Bible in Amharic since 1828.

Great bar bet information. Actually, it's for serious scholars, but knuckleheads can enjoy it, too.

Law and Judaism

http://www.tourolaw.edu/institutes/jewishlaw/december95/toc.html

Law and Judaism meet in the reports of Touro Law School's *Jewish Law Reports*. Touro is located in New York City. You'll find discussions on topics ranging from the O.J. trial to "Is Playing the Lottery Permissible Under Jewish Law?" Full texts of symposium discussions.

Martin Buber

http://www.rz.uni-karlsruhe.de/~uneu/bubere.htm

The great 20th-century philosopher of Judaism, Martin Buber, would be pleased with this home page dedicated to his life and thought. This one's in English; you'll find a more complex version in German at the same location.

Peace Agreement

http://www.jpost.co.il/Oslo2/

The text of the accords signed on the White House lawn by Arafat and Rabin; from the *Jerusalem Post*.

Polygamy in Jewish History

http://www.hal.com/~landman/Poly/je2.html

A brief history of the attitudes toward polygamy in Jewish law.

Responses to Christian Missionaries

http://www.utexas.edu/students/cjso/untitled_folder/Truth_page.html

From the University of Texas, a scholar offers suggestions on how to handle Christian missionaries. Christian vs. Jewish understandings of scripture, "How to Talk to a Missionary," and tons more.

Samaritans

ftp://ftp.lehigh.edu/pub/listserv/ioudaios-l/Articles/lgsamar

Who are the Samaritans, also known as the *Shomronim?* Learn about them in this scholarly article by Lester L. Grubbe of the University of Hull, England.

Ten Plagues

http://www.plaguescape.com/

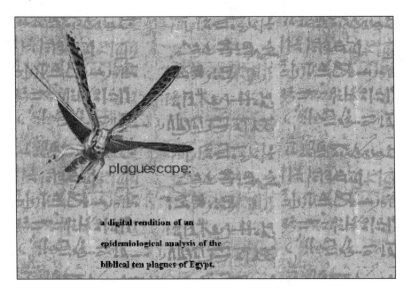

plaguescape:

a digital rendition of an
epidemiological analysis of the
biblical ten plagues of Egypt.

Scientific explanations for the 10 plagues in the Exodus story, conveyed with warmth, wit, and weblinks. Also a sophisticated bibliography, maps, and the when, where, and who of it all.

Tiberian Segols

http://oi.uchicago.edu:1080/pub/papers/goerwitz/sbl94talk/sbl94talk.html

If you're anything like me, and my therapist hopes you aren't, this question has been keeping you up late at night, too. The question, of course, is this: Is the "segol" in Tiberian Hebrew a phoneme? Or is it a candy? Or a gum? This is actually a serious website, a discussion of Hebrew linguistics, but you could never tell from this description.

CHAPTER SIXTEEN

FOR SALE

THE INTERNET IS A FASCINATING new marketing tool. Advertisers can present reams of information, as well as photos, video, sound, and all sorts of other material about their products. The tricky thing is getting you, the potential customer, to visit the site. Purveyors of Jewish art, food, religious objects, books, music, and more are already standing by in cyberspace. Most of the sites below contain order forms—you can buy things over the Net with a credit card.

If you have written a book, you will find the Internet an intriguing way to promote—and sell—your work. Take a look at the websites for specific books listed below.

As with any other mail order opportunity, buyer beware: Anyone can put up a website. The **NOTE** publisher of *The Guide to the Jewish Internet* reminds you that the listings in this section are simply a service to the reader. We do not in any way vouch for the authenticity of the sellers.

These sites are representative of what's out there. If we didn't review your site, either we couldn't find it or we found others that were similar enough.

Having said that, let's whip out our MasterCards and go shopping.

ArtScroll

http://www.artscroll.com/

ArtScroll is a large and well-respected publisher of Jewish texts, commentaries, and biographies. You'll find translations and texts of everything from the Bible to the Passover Haggadah, as well as virtually everything in print for the Jewish home. Their webpage is big and therefore a little slow, but worth the wait.

Chai on Life

http://www.csra.net/ronaldr/

Get your challah covers, Hebrew name ties, tie-dyed kippot, and other unique Jewish items here.

Concertina

http://www.iatech.com/books/

Concertina is a Canadian children's publisher, offering print and online versions of its books.

Cyberspace *Shuk*

http://www.cybershuk.com/

Lots of stores, lots of stuff. Art, books, tapes, and lots more. *Shuk*, of course, is the Arabic word for marketplace. "Cyberspace" is the Arabic word for cyberspace.

Esrogim

http://users.aol.com/kingbear/esrog.html

An *esrog* looks like a large, firm, lumpy lemon and plays an important part in Sukkot celebrations. Order yours here.

Feldheim Publishers

http://www.worldplaza.com/aleph1/feldheim/feldheim.html

One of the leaders in Jewish publications offers you a 10% discount on all books purchased over the Internet.

Golden Rules

http://www.scruz.net/~zvi/goldrul1.html

Golden Rules: The Ten Ethical Values Parents Need to Teach Their Children, by Rabbi Wayne Dosick, published by HarperSan Francisco.

Israeli Hebrew Mall/Electronic Shopping Center

http://kenionet.com/kenionet/indexh.html

The Israeli Hebrew Mall/Electronic Shopping Center—you need Hebrew to make sense of this site, and so does your browser.

Jan's Custom Knits

http://www.puffin.com/puffin/index.html

Custom, personalized baby blankets with Hebrew inscriptions. Designs from all over the world.

The Jewish Experience!   RECOMMENDED

http://www.catalog.com/aish/index.htm#Campustr

Aish HaTorah, one of the first and most successful *ba'al teshuva yeshivot*, or Jewish schools seeking to "return" Jews to Judaism, offers a wide variety of tapes and books on religious themes, Judaica, Jewish music, and other items.

Multimedia Judaic Software

http://www.radix.net/~dor_l_dor/Welcome.html

Multimedia Judaic Software teaches you to "Read Hebrew Now" or learn about traditional Jewish blessings; from Dor L'Dor.

Our World

http://ourworld.compuserve.com/homepages/emj/bnai.htm

A Windows program to keep track of Bar and Bat Mitzvah planning. Make sure you don't forget Uncle Saul.

Project Judaica Foundation

http://www.kks.com/pj/default.html

Project Judaica Foundation is a private nonprofit group dedicated to preserving and exhibiting Jewish art and artifacts from around the world. A professional-looking webpage but something of a tease as well—you can order a CD-ROM version of the Dead Sea Scrolls for $54.95 or an original, early American Passover Haggadah for $1,500.

Tefillin: The Inside Story

http://www.t-r-c.com/t-r-c/tefillin/

Tefillin: The Inside Story, from Feldheim Publishers, is a book by Rabbi Moshe Shlomo Emanuel explaining everything to do with the system of leather straps and boxes worn by traditionally minded Jewish males in morning prayer.

Traditions

http://www.dircon.co.uk/traditions/

Traditions offers a wide variety of items with Jewish themes for the holidays, the home, and more.

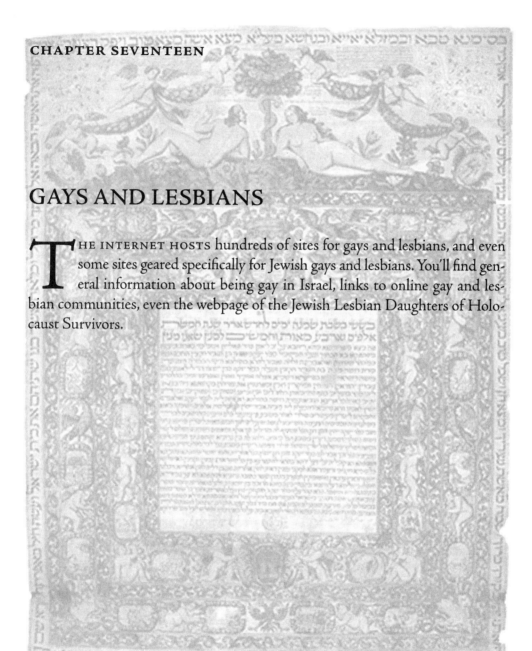

CHAPTER SEVENTEEN

GAYS AND LESBIANS

THE INTERNET HOSTS hundreds of sites for gays and lesbians, and even some sites geared specifically for Jewish gays and lesbians. You'll find general information about being gay in Israel, links to online gay and lesbian communities, even the webpage of the Jewish Lesbian Daughters of Holocaust Survivors.

Gays and Lesbians in Israel

RECOMMENDED

http://www.otago.ac.nz:80/qrd/world/middle_east/israel/

Information and mailing lists regarding gay and lesbian Jews in Israeli society, military, and nightlife. Phone numbers for support and counseling hotlines; facts about AIDS in Israel; gay rights protection in Israel; Passover seder information; clubs, coffeehouses; bookstores; and directions to a gay nude beach.

Jewish Lesbian Daughters of Holocaust Survivors

http://tps.stdorg.wisc.edu/MGLRC/Groups/JewishLesbianDaughtersof.html

This is the home page of the Jewish Lesbian Daughters of Holocaust Survivors, an international networking and support group exclusively for Jewish lesbians, one or both of whose parents survived the Nazi regime. The page explains that the group was formed in 1986 and has membership in five countries on three continents. A contact name and address is provided.

Links

http://www.otago.ac.nz:80/qrd/religion/judeochristian/judaism/

Resources: Some links for gay and lesbian Jews. You'll find "Gay-Jews," a mailing list for lesbian, gay, and bisexual Jews; a gay-lesbian Jewish archive; a list of Jewish pro-gay books; and an article by a mainstream rabbi about homosexuality in Jewish law.

Nice Jewish Girls

http://www.zoom.com/personal/staci/njg.htm

The Nice Jewish Girls Mailing List for lesbian and bisexual women. In addition to the mailing list, you'll find a repository of links to individual women's pages; lesbian and bisexual women are invited to link their pages here. The administrator of the mailing list makes clear that it's strictly for lesbian and bisexual Jewish women.

Queer in Israel

http://qrd.tau.ac.il/

Queer in Israel is the name of a home page with information on Israel's gay community. You'll find links to the Society for the Protection of Individual Rights and the Tel Aviv Gay and Lesbian Center, and updates on gay and lesbian life in Israel.

San Antonio, Texas

http://www.shalom.com/havurah.htm

The San Antonio, Texas, gay Jewish Havurah welcomes you at its home page. You'll find an e-mail address and telephone numbers for further information.

World Congress of Gay & Lesbian Jewish Organizations

http://www.nyu.edu/pages/sls/jewish/wcgljo.html

The World Congress of Gay & Lesbian Jewish Organizations provides lists of constituent groups around the world, lists of relevant mailing lists, usenet newsgroups, and reading lists. A comprehensive website.

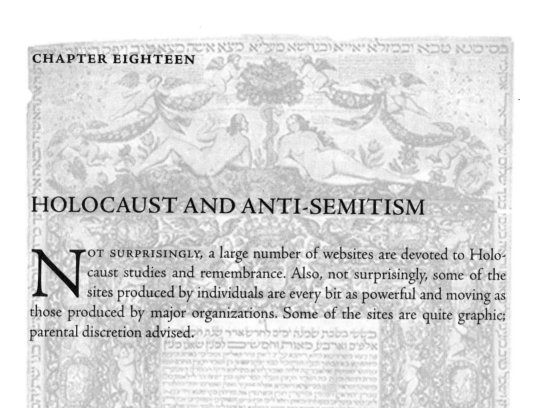

CHAPTER EIGHTEEN

HOLOCAUST AND ANTI-SEMITISM

NOT SURPRISINGLY, a large number of websites are devoted to Holocaust studies and remembrance. Also, not surprisingly, some of the sites produced by individuals are every bit as powerful and moving as those produced by major organizations. Some of the sites are quite graphic; parental discretion advised.

AMCHA Home

http://www.jer1.co.il/orgs/amcha/amcha1.htm

A charitable organization offering support to Holocaust survivors and their families. Read back issues of their newsletter and contact them by e-mail here.

Anne Frank

http://www.glyphs.com/millpop/95/annfrank.html

A thoughtful essay, published in millennium pop, on Anne Frank's *Diary of a Young Girl*. Sara Laschever is the author.

Anne Frank Center USA

http://www.annefrank.com/

Dedicated to the preservation of the famous Holocaust diarist's memory, the Anne Frank Center USA offers the story behind the diary; an online visit to the Annex, the secret chamber where Anne and her family lived; a scrapbook picture history of Anne's life; and background information about her diary. You can read about Anne's story, and you'll also find a short history of the Holocaust. There's also information about "Anne Frank in the World: 1929–1945," a traveling exhibit. The bookstore offers various editions of the diary as well as publications from the Anne Frank house.

Anti-Defamation League

http://www.adl.org/

The Anti-Defamation League (ADL) fights anti-Semitism through programs and services that counteract hatred, prejudice, and bigotry. Visit their site, filled with vital, up-to-the-minute information about anti-Semitism in the U.S., both on campus and worldwide. Read the latest ADL reports and search by subject. For example, when I visited the site and went to the ADL Focus menu, I found topics such as hate crimes, the Nation of Islam, militia groups, the college campus, and more. The Nation of Islam file describes Minister Louis Farrakhan's use of anti-Semitism in order to build his stature in the black community. The militia section shows how militia leaders target Jews and disseminate the notorious "Protocols of the Elders of Zion."

Art Spiegelman's *Maus*

http://jefferson.village.virginia.edu/holocaust/spiegelman.html

Maus is a phenomenally powerful graphic novel by Art Spiegelman. With links to scholarly and related Holocaust references.

Auschwitz: A German Resource

http://www.wsg-hist.uni-linz.ac.at/Auschwitz/HTML/Seite1.html

A resource on Auschwitz, in German. While I don't read German, the simple fact that this page exists, in German, intrigues me.

Auschwitz: A Layman's Guide

http://www.almanac.bc.ca/faqs/auschwitz/index.html

Auschwitz in detail. From essays by Ken McVay. Includes geographic descriptions, grim facts about methods of extermination and medical experimentation, and a wide variety of subjects. Topics include gas chambers, Zyklon B, crematoria, and compiling the estimates on numbers exterminated.

Auschwitz Alphabet

http://www.spectacle.org/695/ausch.html

A harrowing, well-written and well-researched A to Z introduction to life and death at Auschwitz. Very powerful. Superb.

Bulgarian Jewry: Salvation of Bulgarian Jews during WW II

http://ASUdesign.eas.asu.edu/places/Bulgaria/Jewish/

The rescue of the Bulgarian Jewish community during World War II is the subject of this Internet archive. You'll find an article about Bulgaria from the Encyclopedia of the Holocaust, an excerpt from Hannah Arendt's *Eichmann in Jerusalem*, symposia, essays, and remembrances.

Cyber Fascism

http://www.mg.co.za/mg/news/nov17-fascists.html

CYBER-FASCISTS ON THE MARCH is the headline of this news story from the *Toronto Globe and Mail* newspaper. Learn how neo-Nazis and racist groups are "spinning a busy web of hate on the Internet." With links to related sites and resources.

Cybrary of the Holocaust

http://remember.org/

A vast amount of information, recollections, essays, photographs, poems, audio interviews you can listen to, and book excerpts concerned with the Holocaust. Including a "virtual tour of Auschwitz." Here you'll find sections dedicated to facts, witnesses, and historical perspectives and study. The facts section includes an extensive and thorough instructional guide to the Holocaust by Gary Grobman covering topics like stereotypes and prejudices, who are the Jews?, Adolf Hitler, and modern anti-Semitism.

Fortunoff Video Archive for Holocaust Testimonies

http://www.library.yale.edu/testimonies/homepage.html

Fortunoff Video Archive for Holocaust Testimonies, Yale University

The Fortunoff video archive is a collection of over 3,500 video-taped interviews with witnesses and survivors of the Holocaust. This website offers sobering text, sound, and video excerpts from the archive. The only downside to this site is that without a very fast Internet connection it will take seemingly forever to download and play any of the video or audio excerpts.

The Holocaust: An Historical Summary

http://www.ushmm.org/education/history.html#two

An excellent starting point for anyone interested in the facts of the Nazi Holocaust. Well worth reading; a great resource for students; a great resource for anyone. Text only. Produced by the United States Holocaust Memorial Museum in Washington, D.C.

The Holocaust Album

http://www.hooked.net/users/rgreene

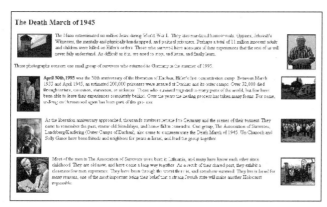

Historical and contemporary photographs, collected by Ron Greene. You'll find photos of a group of survivors who returned to Germany in 1995, remembrance of the 1945 death march, and "Visas for Life," the story of a Japanese diplomat who violated government orders and risked his own life to save 6,000 Jews. Beautifully designed and displayed; quite moving. The photos download slowly, but they're worth the time it takes.

Holocaust Memorial, Miami Beach, Florida

http://wahoo.netrunner.net/~holomem/

A virtual tour of the attractively designed, art-filled, and moving Holocaust Memorial Garden of Miami Beach, Florida. "In 1985, Kenneth Treister was commissioned to design a memorial to the Jewish culture and the individuals killed in the Holocaust. The Memorial Garden gives survivors and mourners a place to visit in lieu of the cemetery they do not have. It expresses in photographs and sculpture the history of the Holocaust so future generations will never forget."

Holocaust Organizations

http://www.ushmm.org/uia-bin/uia_list/sites.lst

A list of Holocaust organizations, with weblinks, sponsored by the United States Holocaust Museum in Washington, D.C.

Holocaust Pictures Exhibition

http://modb.oce.ulg.ac.be/schmitz/holocaust.html

Francois Schmitz has performed a vital service for students of the Nazi Holocaust. He has downloaded and reformatted 37 powerful and dramatic photographs that had been hidden away in two gopher menu files, added explanatory text, and put the whole thing together for you with an index that depicts the brutal nature of the photographs. Examples: two Jewish pupils humiliated before their classmates; German soldiers brutalizing an elderly Jew in Poland; a mass execution of Jews in the Nazi-occupied Soviet Union. Obviously, not for the faint of heart.

Holocaust Rescuers   RECOMMENDED

http://www.cs.cmu.edu/afs/cs.cmu.edu/user/mmbt/www/rescuers.html

An extremely lengthy annotated bibliography of works honoring those who rescued Jews and others during the Nazi Holocaust. An excellent resource for researchers, students, and authors.

Holocaust Resources (continued)

http://www.charm.net/~rbennett/links.html

An impressive, annotated listing of Holocaust resources on the Web, by Hero of the Jewish Internet Robert J. Bennett. Hero Bennett has visited each site and provides you with a brief explanation of what you'll find there and why each site is worth your time.

Holocaust Studies Center

http://www.bxscience.edu/orgs/holocaust/index.html

The Holocaust Studies Center, at the Bronx High School of Science, was founded in 1978 and is one of the first such institutions in the United States. The Center seeks to maintain awareness of the lessons of the Holocaust. High school students in particular will enjoy this site, although the tone and content are for adults as well.

HWEB Project

http://www.almanac.bc.ca/hweb/

Here's a resource to keep your eye on. Thanks to the Herculean efforts of Hero of the Jewish Internet Ken McVay, over 4,000 text-only files containing information about the Holocaust and the rise of modern-day fascism will soon become available to Internet users. The files reside at the FTP (file transfer protocol) server of Nizkor, a Holocaust remembrance organization. Volunteers are needed to help prepare the files for Internet accessibility. If you'd like to learn more about the project, or, better still, volunteer your time, contact the project managers here.

The Janusz Korczak Living Heritage Association

http://www.hls.se/ped/korczak/

Janusz Korczak, a Polish nursery school operator, perished with the children in his care. Meet this Gentile martyr at the home site of the Janusz Korczak Living Heritage Association. Photos, a bibliography, a chronicle of his life, and more about the man they call the "King of Children."

L'Chaim: A Holocaust Web Project

http://www.charm.net/~rbennett/l'chaim.html

This website offers a virtual tour of Dachau, including photos and testimonials from survivors. Dachau, constructed on the site of an old munitions factory, was the first concentration camp in Germany. Many of its prisoners were forced to work in German factories in nearby Munich, while others were used as human guinea pigs in experiments. By clicking on a map of Dachau, you can visit the various parts of the camp and read about what happened at each site. Leave your thoughts on Dachau on the L'Chaim Response Page. Home page of Robert J. Bennett, Hero of the Jewish Internet.

I*EARN Holocaust/Genocide Project

http://www.peg.apc.org/~iearn/hgpproject.html

The Holocaust/Genocide Project from I*EARN of Australia offers an electronic conference and gopher menus focused on the Holocaust. The conference offers information "unique and exclusively for I*EARN participants." This includes interviews with survivors and rescuers, discussion groups, and support for students and teachers. The gopher menus (gopher://gopher.igc.apc.org:7009/1) include historic time lines, bibliographical and resource materials on the Holocaust, a Poland-Israel study mission, and *An End to Intolerance*—a student magazine.

In Lieu of Flowers

http://www.wam.umd.edu/~drmaier/inlieu.html

Excerpts from the book *In Lieu of Flowers*, by Louis Maier; 28 stories about life in the small German town of Malsch as the Nazis came to power.

Leni Riefenstahl

http://rubens.anu.edu.au/riefenstahl/

Black-and-white still photographs from filmmaker Leni Riefenstahl's monumental films about the Nazi era in Germany, *Triumph of the Will* (1934) and *Olympiad* (1936). *Triumph of the Will* depicts a mass Nazi rally; *Olympiad* focuses on the 1936 Berlin Summer Olympics. From the Australian National University; in both JPG and GIF formats.

Louisiana Holocaust Survivors' Home Page

http://www.tulane.edu/~so-inst/laholsur.html

Survivors living in Louisiana share their stories of survival in several very personal, moving interviews at this Tulane University site.

Maurice Mendjisky

http://orangeraie.azur.fr/mm1_e.htm

Maurice Mendjisky, Polish artist and friend of Picasso and Marc Chagall, drew powerful and moving sketches of the Warsaw Uprising. Meet the artist here. With links to a French Riviera museum that displays his work.

The Mechelen Museum of Deportation and the Resistance

http://www.cicb.be/shoah/

The Mechelen Museum of Deportation and the Resistance, also known as the Shoah (Holocaust) Museum, records the effects of the Holocaust in Belgium in this sensitive, well-written, and well-designed home page. Nearly half of the Jews of Belgium were killed in the Holocaust. Here you'll read about Jewish life before the Holocaust, anti-Semitism and the rise of Nazism, Belgium under Nazi occupation, the Hundred Days of 1942, and the entire history of the war through the Liberation.

Museum of Tolerance, Los Angeles   RECOMMENDED

http://www.wiesenthal.com/mot/index.html

The Simon Wiesenthal Center's Museum of Tolerance is a high tech, hands-on experiential museum that focuses on two themes through unique interactive exhibits: the dynamics of racism and prejudice in America, and the history of the Holocaust. Visit it here, where you can learn about children of the Holocaust, upcoming lectures and exhibits, even take an online tour. Lots to read and learn. The essay information included in the online tour would be especially useful for younger students.

RECOMMENDED

Nizkor Project (Holocaust Archive)

http://www.nizkor.eye.net/

"Truth is far more fragile than fiction. Reason alone cannot protect it." This quotation from Deborah Lipstadt's work *Denying the Holocaust* introduces the home page of the Nizkor Project. Nizkor offers a variety of projects, all of which draw attention to those who deny the Nazi Holocaust. An extremely vital resource, the Nizkor Project provides responses to frequently asserted statements by Holocaust deniers; a layman's guide to issues surrounding Holocaust denial; thousands of files with Holocaust information available via FTP; and much more. An outstanding site, worthy of your time, whether you are a Holocaust scholar or an individual who wants to learn more.

Nysernet Holocaust Resources

gopher://israel.nysernet.org:71/11/holocaust/
gopher://israel.nysernet.org:70/11/israel/iis/hol

Nysernet offers a couple of gopher menus that aid Holocaust study. The first offers a short statistical summary of the Holocaust by German historians, with excerpts from Nazi documents, information on neo-Nazis, and more. The second links to sites like the Holocaust and Holocaust Denial Archives.

"Protocols of the Elders of Zion"   RECOMMENDED

gopher://ftp.std.com/11/obi/book/Rants/Protocols

Learn all about the notorious anti-Jewish tract "The Protocols of the Elders of Zion" at this gopher site. The Protocols first surfaced in Russia in 1905, purporting to document a Zionist conspiracy to take over the world. Hitler relied on the document when writing *Mein Kampf*; anti-Semites have spread it around for almost a century. An excellent essay; also, quotes from various individuals like Henry Ford, who in 1921 wrote, "The only statement I care to make about the Protocols is that they fit in with what is going on. They are sixteen years old and they have fitted the world situation up to this time. They fit it now."

Raoul Wallenberg   RECOMMENDED

http://www.algonet.se/~hatikva/wallenberg/

A well-written website commemorating Swedish diplomat Raoul Wallenberg, who single-handedly saved the lives of 30,000 to 100,000 Hungarian Jews during the Holocaust only to be arrested, at the war's end, by the Soviets.

But what became of this extraordinary World War II hero? Was he put to death or, as reports had it, was he imprisoned in the Soviet gulag or in a Soviet psychiatric hospital? Learn the answer here. You'll also find photographs, including an image of one of the passes he procured that brought Jews to safety.

Reach & Teach

http://pages.prodigy.com/AZ/kinder/Holocausteducation.html

A resource for Holocaust education. The Reach & Teach group consists of Holocaust survivors, their families, and Jewish educators across the United States. They seek to inform Jews and non-Jews about the Holocaust, and they use the Internet and school visits to deliver their message. They are available to speak at your school on a variety of subjects (listed at their site) related to the rise and fall of Nazi Germany and to the Holocaust.

RECOMMENDED

Remembering the Holocaust

http://werple.mira.net.au/~aragorn/holocaus.html

An extremely thorough annotated listing of Holocaust resources on the Web, together with hyperlinks to the various sites. This is a great place from which to begin your exploration, since you'll find links to the Yad Vashem Holocaust memorial in Israel, the U.S. Holocaust Museum, the Nizkor Project, and more.

Responses to the Holocaust

http://jefferson.village.virginia.edu/holocaust/response.html

"Responses to the Holocaust: A Hypermedia Sourcebook for the Humanities" is a project of the University of Virginia. Some aspects are still under construction, but you will eventually find the Holocaust in literature, literary criticism and theory, philosophy, history, poetry, film, psychoanalysis, sociology, and art and architecture. Soon to be a massive scholarly resource.

Shoah Visual History Foundation

http://www.turner.com/survivors/SVHF.html

Steven Spielberg has started the "Survivors of the Shoah Visual History Foundation." Here you can learn about the technical aspects of recording thousands of survivors' stories.

Social Studies School Service

http://www.socialstudies.com/holo.html

Resources on Holocaust studies for schoolteachers. Descriptions and ordering opportunities for books, videos, photos, and more from Social Studies School Service.

Time Line

gopher://gopher.igc.apc.org:7009/11/time-lines

A useful time line related to the Holocaust. Events from 1919 through 1945 are covered in a clear and concise manner. From the I*EARN Holocaust/Genocide Project gopher. A good starting point for students; about six pages of text.

United States Holocaust Memorial Museum   RECOMMENDED

http://www.ushmm.org/

Pay a cybervisit to this extraordinary collection, museum, library, and learning center focused on the Holocaust. A search engine allows you to access many of the museum's resources from your home. Facts, statistics, online education, conferences—this is an awesome website. A query system allows you to enter words or phrases and discover related material in the archives of the museum. Transcripts of lectures and symposia at the museum are available online, some in text and some via audio. You can also hear camp songs—music written by inmates of concentration camps. A videography for educators includes hundreds of video resources described by topic and appropriate age group. And much more. A website beyond compare.

Vancouver Holocaust Centre

http://hoshi.cic.sfu.ca/~spec-state/vhec.html

The basics about the Vancouver Holocaust Centre, which acts as a resource for teachers and students learning about the Holocaust.

Vidal Sassoon International Center for the Study of Anti-Semitism

http://www2.huji.ac.il/www_jcd/about.html

The Sassoon International Center for the Study of anti-Semitism, based at Hebrew University in Jerusalem and founded in 1982, offers cyberresearchers an online bibliography of works concerned with anti-Semitism and the Holocaust. You'll also find abstracts of articles, information about publications and courses, research projects, online databases, and an analysis of current trends in anti-Semitism. An extremely useful resource for the serious student.

The Wolf Lewkowicz Collection

http://web.mit.edu/afs/athena.mit.edu/user/m/a/maz/wolf/

This is a collection of 178 moving and emotional letters, written between 1922 and 1939, by a Polish Jew to his American nephew. The original letters, in Yiddish, are at Harvard; the English translations are here. Wolf Lewkowicz died in Treblinka in 1943; he was 56 years old. Letter 179, written by two of his nephews in 1945 from what was then Palestine, contains a description of Wolf's final, tortured days.

World War II Newsgroup

news:soc.history.war.world-war-ii"

This World War II–focused newsgroup discusses topics such as Zyklon B, bombing of concentration camps, and who contributed most to the defeat of Nazi Germany.

Yad Vashem

http://www.yad-vashem.org.il/

Explanations of facilities, descriptions of exhibits, and an exhibition of photos are what you'll find on Yad Vashem's home page, Israel's Holocaust memorial, museum, and library.

CHAPTER NINETEEN

ISRAEL

IF IT'S HAPPENING NOW IN ISRAEL, or if it happened any time in the last 4,000 years, you can find it on the Internet. In this section you'll find online addresses for everything in Israel, from fine wines to radio stations, from universities to theaters, from low culture to high culture, from kibbutzim to information on how to make aliyah. If you're planning a trip to Israel, you'll discover all sorts of people, places, and things to enhance your visit. If you're doing research or a school paper, you'll get all the information you need on virtually any topic connected with the Holy Land. Enjoy.

Israel: An Internet Overview

Aliyah

http://www.jer1.co.il/aliyah/

The World Zionist Organization offers a thorough guide to the process of aliyah—of moving to Israel.

Aliyah is the Hebrew word meaning "to go up," and Jews have traditionally believed that moving from anywhere else on earth to the Holy Land is a spiritual step up. But such a move is fraught with complications like army service, dual nationalities, tax issues, moving households, and finding employment, just to name a few. This website gets you started on the way up.

Everything Israel

gopher://israel-info.gov.il/

An up-to-the-minute encyclopedia of everything Israel. Politics, archeology, economics, Israeli news, maps and pictures, anti-Semitism, and the Holocaust—every question you've got about Israel has an answer here. All by itself, this gopher menu provided by the Israeli government is reason enough to convince parents to get hooked onto the Web—and to hook up their kids, too.

Kibbutzim

http://www2.NetVision.net.il/~selamo/#other

A list of kibbutzim on the Internet, with hyperlinks, thoughtfully provided by Kibbutz Cabri, located in northern Israel. Forty-six kibbutzim are listed. You'll find links to their home pages, to one-paragraph summary descriptions, or to reports by recent guests. Some of the kibbutzim offer bed and breakfast; others, archeological digs; still others, volunteer opportunities. It's still Israel, so not all of the links actually connect to anything, but it's certainly a noble effort to pull together information that used to be extremely difficult to find quickly.

The New Jerusalem Mosaic

http://snunit.huji.ac.il/njeru/open_screen2.htm

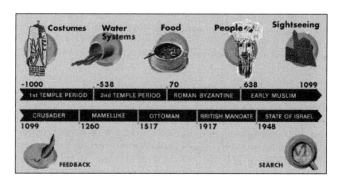

You'll enter the Jerusalem Mosaic and you'll never want to leave. The history of Jerusalem in text, photos, and maps, with information on food, water, costumes, politics, everything. Beautifully and thoughtfully designed. Great for kids. Takes full advantage of hypertext technology. Hats off to Hebrew University for this wonderful, mind-expanding site.

Ruth Gonzalez

http://www.walla.co.il/online/allstars/index.html

Enough intellectual stuff. Ruth Gonzalez is the host of Israel's *Wheel of Fortune*, and this is her website. She likes singing, spaghetti, reading, pets, dancing, shopping, and cooking. She hates traffic jams, fake people, humidity, liars, snobs, airports, crowded places, and waiting on line. She is thoughtfully posed leaning forward in front of a panel truck.

Wines in Israel

http://server.agmonet.co.il/~wine/

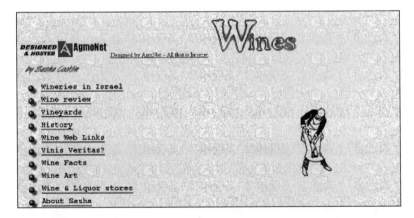

Wines in Israel home page, by Sasha Cooklin, offers a heady bouquet of information about wineries in Israel (including touring opportunities), wine weblinks, reviews, history, and wine facts. Very imaginative and useful site.

Broadcasting

Arutz 7

http://www.jer1.co.il/media/arutz7/index.html

Arutz 7 is Israel's only independent radio station. Its valuable webpage presents today's news and opinion, a digest of news from the Arab press, and a feature called "Good News from Israel."

Israel Educational Television

http://www.ventura.co.il/e/edutv/start.htm

Founded in 1966, Israel Educational Television (IET) brings highbrow culture to Israelis, who, of course, watch *Baywatch* reruns. Can you blame them? Seriously, you can order videos of Israeli educational shows. Categories include early childhood, teaching language, the Israel scene, and Bagrut programs.

Israel Television

http://tvnet.com/tv/il/il.html

Who shows what on Israeli TV? Find out here with this listing of Israeli television and cable TV stations. You'll also find a link to the "Ultimate TV List," a great resource for Israeli television programming information if you're living in Israel and a total TV addict.

Kol Israel

http://ayalon.eng.tau.ac.il/~oded/iarc-files/kol-israel

Kol Israel Radio's international broadcasting schedule. From the Israel Amateur Radio Club. Everything that you can think of for amateur radio types: a QSL bureau, classes, licenses, contests, and a plea to protect amateur radio. Hey, can I ask a stupid question? Can you have "ham" radio in Israel? A "QSL card," incidentally, is what amateur radio operators request from radio stations around the world that they pick up via shortwave. When I was growing up, it was a big deal to buy a ham radio kit, solder all the wires and doodads together, string out an antenna around some trees, and fire it up. Getting a radio station from Ecuador or Budapest was a very big deal. I suppose the Internet is going to replace that; something's lost, though. Those interested in amateur radio should visit the Israel Amateur Radio Club at its website, http://ayalon.eng.tau.ac.il/~oded/iarc.htm.

Reshet Gimmel

http://teletel.co.il/gimmel/index.html

The home page of broadcasting's Reshet Gimmel, an Israeli radio station, with news about the shows and the music. With imaginative spelling. You can also listen to sound tracks, jingles, "and other cool stuff," take a "top 20 quiz" and "win many prizes," and "go back stage" to read the biographies of the on-air personalities. Hey, it's just for fun.

Culture

Eshkolot

http://shani.net/eshkolot/

Eshkolot is the Israeli Artistes' Company for Performers' Rights. The group, with more than 2,000 Israeli singers, dancers, and other performers, seeks to protect its members' rights, especially in an era of burgeoning technologies. Soon to have links to members' home pages. Also provides links to "copyright-concerned Internet links." Of interest more to performers than audiences. Roughly the equivalent of the American ASCAP organization.

Israel National Museum of Science

http://www.elron.net/n_sci_museum/

This museum, located at the Technion Institute in Haifa, offers cybervisitors a peek at current exhibitions, information about its history, overviews of different installations, and a guide to its youth programs. While not a virtual tour, this site will give you a feeling for the scope of the museum. You'll find a few interesting photos along with a brief description of one current exhibition. A recent example: "Radio: The Early Days."

Sabra Music Center

http://SABRAnet.com

The Sabra Music Center, "Where Israel comes alive on the Internet," offers short, downloadable excerpts from Israeli pop songs from the 60s, 70s, 80s, and 90s. Also a chat room and a pretty extensive list of Israel-related links. **Note:** They suggest you download a version of Internet Wave (you'll find a link at the site) in order to hear the sound files.

Tmu-Na Theatre

http://www.pf1.co.il/tmu-na/

Tmu-Na Theatre of Tel Aviv offers workshops and plays; get to know the company and its offerings here. Tmu-Na was established in 1981 by Nava Zuckerman to provide artists working in theater, movies, music, painting, and creative writing with "the opportunity to develop and express their personal skills in a multi-disciplinary environment." Talk about a group that could really make phenomenal use of the Internet. I'd love to see videos of their plays and examples of the painting and creative writing. So would theatergoers. What a great way to boost interest and sell tickets. And speaking of tickets, you can make reservations online and enjoy a 25% discount.

Education

Education in Israel

gopher://israel.nysernet.org:70/11/israel/iis/edu

At this gopher site you'll find links to information about education in Israel, such as facts and figures about education and culture in Israel, student programs in Israel, the Jewish student university network, student activist groups and student information, the Joint Authority for Jewish Zionist Education, profiles of Israeli high schools with e-mail, youth movements and organizations in Israel, and more.

Hebrew University

http://www1.huji.ac.il

The home page of the Hebrew University of Jerusalem. Learn about the campus and its various departments, search several libraries and databases in Hebrew and English (located both in and out of Israel). This is also the home of the new and old Jerusalem Mosaic projects (a terrific, virtual tour through Jerusalem past and present), as well as other, similar educational projects. This is a wonderful site with lots of information and educational material.

The Open University of Israel

http://www.openu.ac.il/

See "Colleges and Universities" for more about this site.

Tel Aviv University

http://www.tau.ac.il/

Tel Aviv University's home page. Contact their various departments and information servers. Not much to look at if you're not part of the university.

Weizmann Institute

http://www.weizmann.ac.il/

See "Colleges and Universities" for more about this site.

And More...

American Physicians Fellowship for Medicine in Israel

http://204.249.224.16:80/~apf/

The American Physicians Fellowship for Medicine in Israel supports the Israeli medical community with fellowships for Israelis in the U.S. and Canada and in other ways as well. Learn about them here.

Canadians in Israel

http://www.ncf.carleton.ca/freeport/government/embassies/mid.east/israel/menu

Canadians in Israel is the topic of this page, presented by the Israeli Embassy in Ottawa. A nice resource for networking.

Comedy Store

http://www.macom.co.il/Channel2/ComedyStore/index.html

The Comedy Store in Israel. Because this site has a lot of graphics, it took a long, long, long time to download; maybe you'll have more luck—and laughs—than I did.

El Al Israel Airlines

http://www.elal.co.il/

Routes, fares, schedules, and little more from Israel's airline. I wonder if you can special-order a nonkosher meal on El Al? What would that be like? Oh, I know: "Will Mr. McGillicuddy identify himself to the flight crew?" Just kidding.

Globes—Employment

http://www.globes.co.il:80/Abroad/abroad.html

This page from Globes Arena, an Israeli Internet company, provides information for Israelis abroad about employment opportunities, military service, customs, and more.

IBM

http://www.ibm.net.il/

Potentially a major resource, because IBM is, well, big. Right now the site's just a cyberbaby, offering links (at this writing) to a few dozen businesses, cultural institutions, and government sites. It also includes a Web phonebook and a list of all Internet domains in Israel. But I'm sure IBMers are circulating around the Holy Land signing up more entities for their sites. Which means that this could be a valuable resource down the road.

Internet in Israel

gopher://israel-info.gov.il:70/11/gophers/internet

The Israeli Government's FAQ about the Internet in Israel. For propellerheads only.

Israel by Gopher

gopher://israel.nysernet.org:70/11/israel

The gopher menu from Nysernet. You'll find links to other gopher menus with hotels, aliyah information, politics in Israel, Jewish/Israeli politics, business and economics, and scientific research and development.

Israel Xpress

http://www.ix.co.il/

This commercial site offers a diverse and interesting range of links to a wide variety of Israeli websites. You'll find links to free on-line media and museums as well as commercial sites focused on tourism, finance, high technology, and products and services.

King Solomon

http://www.demon.co.uk/solbaram/articles/fn2.html

An interesting essay on Israel in the time of King Solomon. Biblical archeology has shed much light on the period following the Jews' entrance into Israel under Joshua and the splitting of the land of Israel into two kingdoms. Learn why that split happened; learn also about the Maccabean dynasty and the events surrounding the Chanukah story.

Livnot U'Lehibanot

http://www.cybergate.net/~livnot/index.html

Livnot U'Lehibanot means "to build and to be built." Livnot is a hiking, work, and study program, conducted in English, in Tsfat and Jerusalem, for Jews aged 21 to 30 with little or no Jewish background. Programs include building projects and community service. Livnot offers an intense course of study in Jewish history as well as Jewish philosophy, holidays, and customs. Weekly hikes are conducted throughout the country. Visit their photo gallery for a constantly changing picture of Livnot projects.

Lotto

http://www.artificia.com/html/lotototo.htm

Lottery results from Israel. Aren't you glad you own a big expensive computer?

Monkey Park

http://www.inter.net.il/monkey_park/monkey_park.html

Now there are *two* places in Israel to see primatelike behavior. One, of course, is the Knesset. The other is Monkey Park, halfway between Jerusalem and Tel Aviv in the Beth Shemen forest. Twenty species of primates and not one calling for early elections.

Shaare Zedek Medical Center

http://www.jer1.co.il/orgs/shaare/shaindex.htm

The oldest hospital in Israel offers its history and seeks your financial support.

CHAPTER TWENTY

ISRAEL—BUSINESS

U P-TO-THE-MINUTE INFORMATION is one of the keys to business suc-
cess. The Internet is an invaluable tool for those seeking to do business
with Israeli firms and for those Israeli firms seeking foreign markets,
partners, and capital. Thanks to the Internet, the business-minded individual
can quickly find information that might have been very difficult to obtain or not
available at all. Search engines, lists of links, news outlets, and government and
trade organizations make doing business with Israel a million times easier.

For example, the United Nations' Trade Point Israel lists dozens of Israeli
companies seeking partnerships outside Israel. The Bezeq White Pages provides contact names, phone numbers, and e-mail addresses for 850 Israeli businesses (so far). The Federation of Israeli Chambers of Commerce provides information—and connections—to thousands of Israeli businesses. And a large
number of Israeli banks, high tech companies, and other firms have established
websites. You can also find search engines to find Israeli businesses, educators,
engineers, or projects that match up with your interests or your company's.

Advanced Technologies in Israel

http://www.matimop.org.il/

The MATIMOP website offers a database describing high tech and industrial projects developed in Israel. You can search for projects by keyword or technological field. MATIMOP is a commercial site that seeks to inform industrial and financial communities around the world of the latest technologies developed in Israel. Businesses can also get assistance in locating potential Israeli research and development partners. I tried the database and searched the word "Internet." I found two related projects. One was an Israeli firm seeking a joint venture partner in order to develop Internet applications. The second involved an Internet data security system an Israeli firm is currently developing.

Amit

http://www.ibm.net.il/amit/

Amit is the Maccabee Workers Union in Israel. An attractive and well-designed website, it offers schedules and information relating to union matters in Hebrew. You'll need software that reads Hebrew in order to make sense of this site—you can read about where to find free downloadable Hebrew font software on page 290.

Bank Leumi

http://www.ventura.co.il/m/meitav/maof/leumi.htm

I think a banker wrote this page. Pretty dry, but if you want to know about this large Israeli bank, the facts are here. Apparently it's a summary of their most recent annual report. What's really wonderful is that they offer you "more information" on charts and graphs. There is exactly one graph. It's in color and it's really pretty. But there's absolutely no explanation of what the graph indicates. I guess it's a display of that subtle banker's sense of humor. On the other hand, if I owned a bank, you think I'd let a bunch of nosy Websurfers find out anything important? Wrong. You want information? Get your own damn bank.

Bezeq White Pages

http://www.bezeq.co.il/WhitePages/

You can look it up: Every Israeli website and e-mail address in one place is the goal of the folks at Bezeq, the Israeli telecom company. At this writing, the listings in this search engine total 850. I tried to look up Scitex, an Israeli high tech company I've heard of. Indeed, I found a phone number, contact person, and an e-mail address. Pretty impressive, and a lot easier than trying to contact directory assistance overseas. They charge about four bucks for that now, incidentally. So check here first.

Computer Jobs in Israel

RECOMMENDED

gopher://gopher.jer1.co.il:70/11/lists/cji

Computer Jobs in Israel offers an exceptionally sensitive and well-written guide to finding high tech employment in the Holy Land. Questions answered include Do I need to know Hebrew to get a computer job in Israel? If I'm still outside Israel, should I send my resume to Israeli companies? How does Russian aliyah and the unemployment rate affect my job search? In addition, over 500 companies list jobs here; you can subscribe for free to CJI and get one to two mailings a week. An excellent service.

Federation of Israeli Chambers of Commerce

RECOMMENDED

http://www.chamber.org.il/

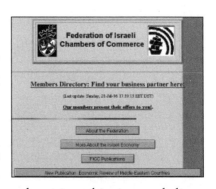

How to connect with thousands of Israeli businesses. From Israel's largest business organization, including among its membership thousands of enterprises in all sectors of the economy—wholesale and retail commerce, export and import trade, manufacturing, finance, banking, real estate, advertising, shipping, and direct marketing. The FICC essentially promotes business in Israel. You'll find information about the Israeli economy, publications like *Economic Review of Middle-Eastern Countries*, a members' communication center, and ways and means by which you can connect with Israeli businesses in your field.

Genesis Business Centers

http://www.interage.co.il/genesis/intro.htm

A source for venture capital for Israeli high tech start-ups and other businesses. Venture capital is an aspect of business that matches investors with, for the most part, new and untried companies. Venturers invest in a variety of new products and ideas with the expectation of making, say, five times their money in five years. Venturers need companies in which to invest; companies need "angels" with capital and connections. Genesis matches the money people with the idea people. This attractive and well-designed website plays the role of corporate *shadchan*, or matchmaker.

RECOMMENDED

Globes

http://www.globes.co.il/

Globes is an Israeli Internet company. They offer as a free service on the Web what they call "Israel's Business Arena." An excellent site with up-to-the-minute information about every aspect of the Israeli economy, from the stock market to real estate, from banking to aviation. Attractive, well organized, easy to use. A super resource. You'll find high tech news, today's financial headlines, the latest news about Israel business, market data, and financial reports.

Innovations

http://www.innovations.co.il/

An excellent online news source focusing on Israeli high technology companies. From the People and Computers Group in Israel. News of Israeli companies, product launches, in-depth analyses of Israeli companies; calendars of business conferences and events. A free and extremely useful business service.

Israel Internet Key

http://www.gold.net.il/~may/may5.htm

Hats off to the folks at Jerusalem-based People and Computers Group, Heroes of the Jewish Internet, who created the Israel Internet Key. They provide, among other things, an excellent list of intriguing Israel-based websites, mostly but not entirely with a science and business bent. Topics include artificial intelligence, aviation, business and commercial, computers, cosmetics, education, engineering, law ... you get the picture.

Israeli Economy

http://www.chamber.org.il/about-economy.html

From the Federation of Israeli Chambers of Commerce comes this brief overview of the Israeli economy. Facts and figures related to business investment, gross domestic product, inflation, and similar matters. The key facts in a single page.

Israeli Government Gopher Menu

gopher://israel-info.gov.il/11/gophers

The Israeli Government maintains this gopher menu connecting you to Israeli universities, an electronic address and phone book, the World Zionist Organization, and Computer Jobs in Israel (CJI). Limited usefulness in that the electronic address book links only to half a dozen institutions, such as Hebrew University or the Weizmann Institute, but it can be worthwhile for you.

Macom

http://www.macom.co.il/whats.new.html

This site connects you to government, business, and commercial websites in Israel. Keep in mind that contacting Israel via the Web takes a little longer than reaching domestic websites. As the Israelis would say, "Savlanut!" Meaning, "Patience!" Actually, what the Israelis say is, "Why don't you move here?"

The Tel Aviv Stock Market

http://www.globes.co.il/

Read all about trading in Israel at this Globes Business Arena page. Stock quotes, company news, latest trends. Woody Allen defines a stockbroker as someone who "invests your money until there's nothing left." Find out how here.

Trade Point Israel

http://www.unicc.org/untpdc/incubator/isr/tptel/

S mall- and medium-sized businesses find information about each other at this United Nations–affiliated website. This is one big website, though: It reached five million hits in early 1996, and the hits just keep on coming. Why? Because businesses can find each other and learn about international trade issues and customs matters, and answer shipping and insurance questions. The U.N. set up Trade Point to help businesses around the world be more competitive and successful by means of the free flow of information. Dozens of Israeli businesses already have linked themselves to this worldwide system.

U.S./Israel Biotechnology Council

http://www.usibc.org/

L earn about biotechnology in Israel at the website of the U.S./Israel Biotechnology Council. The site offers a general overview of Is-rael's biotechnology industry and provides information about Al-liance '96, a conference involving Israeli biotech companies, universi-ties, and research institutions.

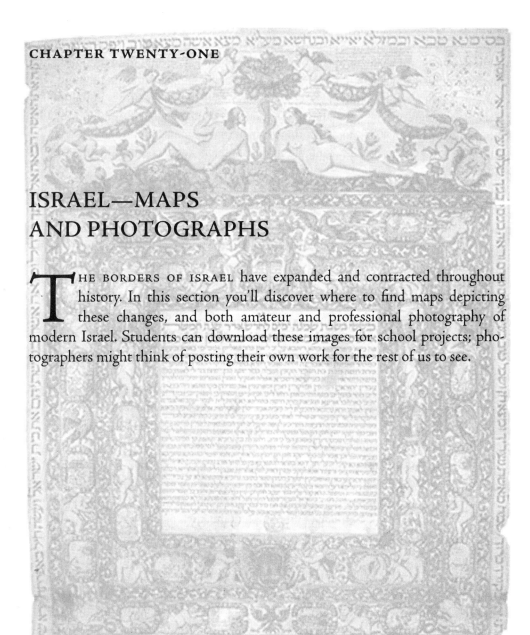

CHAPTER TWENTY-ONE

ISRAEL—MAPS
AND PHOTOGRAPHS

THE BORDERS OF ISRAEL have expanded and contracted throughout history. In this section you'll discover where to find maps depicting these changes, and both amateur and professional photography of modern Israel. Students can download these images for school projects; photographers might think of posting their own work for the rest of us to see.

Caesarea, Israel

http://www.hyperion.com/~koreth/israel/caesarea.html

Steven Grimm takes you on a virtual tour of the ancient seaside Israeli city of Caesarea, known for its Roman theater (still in use today), aqueduct, and history. Great photos at this site download speedily and offer you wonderful views.

Jerusalem

http://www.israel-mfa.gov.il/

Attractive photographs of Jerusalem by professional photographer Shai Ginott. Gorgeous work. From an exhibition traveling the world, sponsored by the Israeli government.

Jerusalem Map

http://www.lib.utexas.edu/Libs/PCL/Map_collection/world_cities/Jerusale.jpg

A map of Jerusalem. This map is big and colorful, but way too big for even a large home computer screen. It's got lots of interesting details, though, so take a look.

RECOMMENDED

Maps of Israeli History

gopher://israel-info.gov.il:70/11/gifs

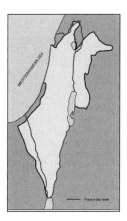

Maps, maps, and more maps of Israel at every point in its history—from cease-fire lines, to the Golan, to ancient history. And these maps are big, beautiful, and in color too (though they may take a long time to download and you probably won't be able to view them all at once on your screen). Who says gopher menus are boring?

Ministry of Tourism Photo Album

http://www.bway.net/israel/israel/israel.html

These photos from the Ministry of Tourism concentrate on the cities and locations that inspired the films in the most recent Israel Film Festival, which is based not in Israel but in New York and Los Angeles. See Jerusalem, Tel Aviv, Haifa, Beersheva, the Dead Sea, Masada, the Kinneret, the Jordan River, and Eilat, among others. Also photos of people and food. If your modem is 28.8 and you're running Netscape, you can take a short automated tour that starts in Jerusalem, takes you to Eilat, and moves you on to the Dead Sea and a wide variety of other vistas. Great fun.

The idea of the Israel Film Festival taking place outside of Israel reminds me of something. I always enjoy seeing Hebrew and Yiddish expressions on "vanity plates" on cars. My all-time favorite is a California plate that says "Rak Shana," which is Hebrew for "Just one year," as in, "Yes, I'm Israeli, and I live in L.A., but I'm only here for just one year." I think it's pretty funny to engrave that expression on a vanity plate.

Photographs of Israel

http://www.leftbank.com/CosWeb/pictures/israel.html#jerusalem

Israel in recent photos, including scenes from Jerusalem, Tel Aviv, Ein Gedi, Caesarea, and Haifa.

WARNING These photos are quite large and may take awhile to download.

Steven Grimm's Photographs

http://www.hyperion.com/~koreth/israel/

Steven Grimm went to Israel in 1992, took great photographs, and loaded them onto his webpage. The next best thing to being there. Mr. Grimm did an excellent job of arranging his photos by area. First you click on the part of Israel you want to visit. Once you've chosen a region, you get interesting, brief descriptions of the areas he's visited. For example, if you go to the Golan Heights, you'll find a transcription of the information pamphlet available at Nimrod's Fortress, one of the largest Crusader fortresses in Israel.

And then when you hit the Golan itself, you see all the photos at once; click on the ones you want to enlarge. This is a great use of the Internet.

CHAPTER TWENTY-TWO

ISRAEL—POLITICS

I N MANY WAYS, Israel is politics—domestic politics, Arab-Israeli relations, U.S.-Israeli affairs. These sites offer up-to-the-minute information on all aspects of Israeli political life. You can tap into the Israeli Foreign Ministry and the embassy in Washington, D.C. You'll find many think tanks and news publications offering essays and articles on timely subjects, all for free, all via the Internet. You can even get information (lots of it) from the CIA and (virtually nothing) from Mossad. Israeli political parties offer websites in English and Hebrew. Think of it as C-Span, about Israel, under your control. They say that if you get 10 Israelis in a room, you'll hear 20 opinions. Why not check out these sites and develop a few hundred opinions of your own.

Academy of Jerusalem

http://www.shamash.org/judaica/acad/

I didn't know what the Academy of Jerusalem is, and now that I've been at their website, I still don't. They, whoever they are, present papers on various aspects of Israeli and Zionist thought. Some of it's pretty loopy, like the "redemptive computer game" in which players "induce" the Palestine Liberation Organization to become a Zionist entity. Some of it's quite good—there are essays by Rabbi Adin Steinsalz, one of the great thinkers of the age. But all in all, I'm glad these guys are on our side. That way we can keep an eye on them.

American Israel Report

http://www.ix.co.il/amir/amir.htm

American Israel Report (AMIR) offers feature articles on politics and economics in Israel. Visit the website to read sample articles such as "Terror Strikes Again," "The Jewish State, Liberal Democracy, and Demographics," "Middle East Peace, Economics, and a Rational Foreign Policy," and "U.S., Israel, and Free Trade." Excellent, well-written essays.

Ariga

http://www.ariga.com/visions/visions.htm

This 'zine focuses on Israeli politics and culture and offers a wide range of extremely interesting material. You'll find poetry, foods of the Bible with expert Phyllis Glazer, Michael Medved on Israeli football, Tel Aviv happenings, and more. *Ariga* is the brainchild of Robert Rosenberg, author and journalist, and offers political and economic news and commentary as well as cultural matters. Well worth your time.

DorShalom

http://www.dorshalom.org.il/

Hebrew for "Generation of Peace," this Israeli group seeks to further the peace process and promote democracy in Israel. The group does not identify itself with any political party. The website offers explanations of the group's objectives, goals, and activities, and offers ways you can volunteer or provide support. You can also listen to the late Israeli prime minister Yitzhak Rabin give his last speech via "audio x-wav."

Elyakim Ha'etzni

http://www.shef.ac.uk/students/md/md911783/haetzni.html

Meet "lawyer, politician, and ideologue" Elyakim Ha'etzni at his website. Ha'etzni is a member of the Israeli Knesset and is involved with issues related to the territories of Judea, Samaria, and the Gaza Strip. Ha'etzni writes frequently for the *Jerusalem Post*, and many of his interesting articles about the peace process are collected here. This website was apparently put together by a British student who shares Ha'etzni's politics.

Facts and Figures from the CIA

http://www.odci.gov/cia/publications/95fact/is.html

The best source for all the facts, figures, names, and places in the State of Israel? Would you believe...the Central Intelligence Agency? Maps, data, environmental information, population statistics, government, economy, transportation, defense forces... and if you can't trust the CIA, then what kind of world are we living in? An excellent overview of the entire State of Israel. And if you access this site before December 31, the CIA promises not to open up a dossier on you or any members of your family! (Just kidding.)

Freeman Center

gopher://gopher.jer1.co.il/11/Politics/research/free

The Freeman Center discusses military and security issues at this gopher menu. Located in Houston, the center says that its primary goal is "to improve Israel's ability to survive in a hostile world. This will be accomplished through research into the military and strategic issues related to the Arab-Israeli conflict and the dissemination of that information to the Jewish community." The group takes the position that Israel needs to preserve Judea, Samaria, Gaza, and the Golan Heights in order to survive. You can read their position papers here.

Golan Heights

http://www.golan.org.il/

Fascinating, urgent website written by the residents of the Golan. The latest news, politics, history, articles, and what you can do to play a role. Again, talk about the Web bringing the Jewish people together. Here you'll find a Golan Heights slide show, facts and figures about the Golan, maps, and information about communities, history, security, relations with Syria, tourism, and water.

Hebron

http://www.jer1.co.il/orgs/communities/hebron/

An excellent opportunity to educate yourself about Jewish history and Israeli politics. Hebron is first mentioned in the book of Genesis after the death of Sarah. Abraham goes there to buy a plot of land for her grave. Thus begins a 4,000-year Jewish involvement in the city, currently the location of a small community of observant Jews surrounded by a much larger group of Arabs. The city's history and role in current Israeli events makes for powerful and often sad reading. Up-to-date interviews with key figures, news stories, history, and photographs make this a website not to be missed.

Information Regarding Israel's Security (IRIS)

http://www.netaxs.com/~iris/

This is an excellent website. Maps, articles, recent quotes from Palestinian leaders, and full texts of key PLO documents make IRIS's case for maintaining a secure Israel. You can subscribe, free of charge, to IRIS's electronic mailing list, which distributes "regular news updates about Israel with a right-of-center slant." For example, one issue of the newsletter contained an English translation of Netanyahu's victory address.

A beautifully designed webpage, with a lot of passion behind it.

Israel Foreign Ministry

http://www.israel-mfa.gov.il/index.html

Home page of the Israel Foreign Ministry. A very exciting place to visit, with current information about Israel, lots of gopher links, explanations of the way the Israeli government works (well, no one can really explain that), speeches, surveys, and peace process documents. This is the Internet equivalent of an Israeli version of C-Span—the government junkie can get lost for hours in here.

Israel-Palestine Center for Research and Information

http://www.pirsonet.co.il/IPCRI/

A think tank jointly run by Jews and Palestinians in Israel offering well-researched, cogent, and well-written articles on the future of the two peoples. Topics include the future of Jerusalem, the issue of water (vital in the Middle East, obviously), economics, law and development, Israeli settlements, and security issues.

Israeli Embassy, Washington, D.C.

http://www.israelemb.org/

The many facets of Israel's touchstone in the American capital. Politics and culture; community outreach including educational, environmental, and interreligious affairs. In the archive you'll find speeches, information about Israel's ambassadors to the U.S., news, and a film archive for educators in the Washington/Virginia/Maryland area. While this site is useful, some of the other entries in this chapter might provide the Netsurfer or student with more information.

Israeli Intelligence Community

http://awpi.com/IntelWeb/Israel/index.html

The barest of facts about the Mossad, Shin Bet, and other members of the Israeli intelligence community. For example, click on Mossad, and you learn that it's the "Agency dedicated to gathering foreign intelligence." You will find its full Hebrew name, former names, names of former heads, and that's about it. I guess if they tell us anything more they'll have to shoot us. I'd love to see more about Mossad in action, or declassified information, or anything. Oh, well.

Israeli Laws

http://www.ix.co.il/

Attorneys and others needing English translations of Israeli laws can order them at this website. This is a commercial site; people who just want a sense of the Israeli legal system can turn to the website of the Israel Foreign Ministry, listed above.

Jerusalem

http://www.gilo.jlm.k12.il/jersa.html

The Jerusalem Municipality, the official name for the City of Jerusalem, promises statistics soon at this home page. At the time of our visit, the site was extremely under construction.

The Jerusalem Insider

http://www.netrail.net/~sidel/insider/insider.html

A political report produced by the Likud party. Extremely current information about the Israeli political scene.

Jerusalem Report

http://www.jreport.virtual.co.il

Excerpts, archives, and subscription information about this bi-weekly newsmagazine. Examples of articles include a recent cover story on the religious revival in Israel and an analysis of Netanyahu's friends in the United States. An archive menu lets you read dozens of articles from the past two years. Quite useful.

Land and Peace

http://www.shef.ac.uk/students/md/md911783/tsow.html

"The Shock of Withdrawal … The State of Israel from the Land of Israel," written by Elyakim Ha'etzni of the Council of Jewish Communities in Judea, Samaria & Gaza. The entire text of a short work condemnatory of the policy of trading land for peace.

Likud Party

http://usa.likud.org.il/index.html

The Likud is the political party of the Israeli right. Its website offers news, views, profiles, and texts related to the peace process, such as a recent Yasir Arafat speech in which Arafat reiterates that his goal is the retaking of Jerusalem. Meet the leaders of the party, see a Likud time line, learn about policy, and get to know new prime minister Benjamin Netanyahu.

Military

ftp://ftp.sunet.se/pub/pictures/history/Israel/military/

Photos and text about Israeli military history here. The images are big and slow to download here, but if you like military history and you've got a little time, then why not tune in? For example, you can see a black-and-white picture from the battle for Jerusalem in 1967 of Israeli troops battling the Jordanians, or a 1955 group photo including Moshe Dayan, Rafael Eitan, Ariel Sharon, and others who went on to leadership positions in the Israeli government.

Missing in Action

gopher://gopher.jer1.co.il:70/11/ped/epa/eng/mia

Israeli soldiers missing in action and the Jewish responsibility to redeem them is the topic of this gopher menu. Aimed at Israeli high school students, the general netcruiser can learn a lot about the way Israel educates—and looks after—her own.

New Israel Fund

http://shamash.nysernet.org/nif/broch.html

The New Israel Fund seeks to increase the level of social justice in the State of Israel. The group focuses on civil and human rights, the role of women, and Arab-Israeli relations. It awards grants in its areas of interest; the website is text only and provides an overview of the Fund's activities.

New Middle East Magazine

http://www.obs-us.com/obs/english/books/mem/obsxxx.htm

The first joint Israeli-Palestinian magazine. A monthly that commenced publication in early 1996, its website offers information about the magazine, articles of interest, and hypertext links to related subjects. Typical subjects: a visit to Palestinian-run Jericho; a comedy team that keeps Jordan laughing; and a Royal Jordanian balloon ride over Wadi Rum. Although there is one article in the current issue entitled "Israeli Politics," by and large the topics focus on Israel's Arab residents and neighbors.

Palestinian Information Center

gopher://alquds.org:70/1

A gopher site managed by the Palestinian Information Center. News and views of history and current political events from the Palestinian point of view. You'll find articles on the "Palestinian Land and People," "Introduction to the Palestinian Cause," Palestinian Organizations and Institutions," and an archive of news and reports.

Peace Now

gopher://shamash.nysernet.org/hh/peace/

Peace Now, Israel's largest grass roots political movement, was founded by 348 former Israeli army officers in 1978. Americans for Peace Now came into existence three years later. The Peace Now website offers you, via gopher, information about the group and essays about the peace process, the issue of the location of the U.S. Embassy in Israel, and the settlements, as well as a selected bibliography.

Primaries

http://www.primaries.co.il/

Political junkies fluent in Hebrew will have a fun time with this site, concerned with primaries in the recent election.

Professors for a Strong Israel

http://www.aquanet.co.il/web/psi/

A "nonpartisan organization of academics" who favor a right-wing approach to Israeli-Arab relations. The website offers the basics about the organization; quotes from David Ben Gurion, one of the founders of Israel; a document archive; and statements to the press. Of primary interest to other like-minded academics.

Tehiya

http://www.shef.ac.uk/students/md/md911783/ehtehiya.html

Tehiya is an Israeli political party fiercely committed to maintaining Israeli control of Judea, Samaria, and Jerusalem. Their webpage offers "Program for the Elections—1988." I don't think there even was a Web in 1988. What's new, folks?

Terrorism

http://shani.net/terror/

The sad facts and frightening photographs of the face of terror in Israel today. Graphic and powerful. These photographs are not for the faint of heart.

U.S. Embassy

http://www.usia.gov/posts/tel_aviv.html

The United States Information Service is a part of the U.S. Embassy in Israel. The webpage offers a lot of basic facts and statistics about Israel and news, presented, of course, with beaucoup diplomatic restraint. Ironically, you'll find a lot more in the CIA website, listed above.

Water

http://menic.utexas.edu/menic/subject/water.html

Water is the subject of this page. You can't make the desert bloom without water, and how the water gets divided is a very important subject in Middle Eastern politics. Soak up knowledge here. Meet MEWIN, the Middle East Water Information Network, where water specialists from many nations meet to "promote the peaceful, cooperative use of this vital resource." Read a "Peace Pipeline" paper related to water issues; and read "Water in the Arab Israeli Peace Process: A Comprehensive Report by the Environment and Conflicts Project," part of the Swiss Peace Foundation. And as they say in Israel, "Save water, shower with a moshav." From the University of Texas's Middle East Network Information Center.

Yisrael Ba-Aliya

http://www.ix.co.il/y_aliya/home.htm

Natan Sharansky, Russian refusenik and Israeli emigre, author of *Fear No Evil*, his account of his time in the Soviet prison system, has founded his own political party in Israel. It actually did fairly well in the recent elections. Read about it here.

Yitzhak Rabin

http://www.israel.org/news/yrabin.html

A biography of Yitzhak Rabin, the late prime minister of Israel, along with speeches, eulogies, and tributes. Provided by the Israeli Ministry of Foreign Affairs.

CHAPTER TWENTY-THREE

ISRAEL—SPORTS

BASKETBALL, SOCCER, AMERICAN FOOTBALL, and more at these sports-crazy websites. Israelis are mad about sports, and the websites dedicated to the various teams reflect their intensity and, frankly, their insanity. The pages, for the most part, are pretty bare, offering little more than schedules, basic statistics, results, standings, and some team history for the more established franchises. They could offer sound, video from recent games, video archives … well, maybe I'm getting a little intense and insane myself.

Beitar Jerusalem Football Club

http://carmel.haifa.ac.il/~ssma599/beitar.html

Read about this famous Israeli soccer team—beaucoup statistics and the history of the club.

Haifa's Team

http://www.yajima.kuis.kyoto-u.ac.jp/staffs/rotter/hapoel/

Tell those Beitar fans where to get off after you visit the unofficial home page of Haifa's team. Meet the president of the team and the current squad. You'll also find the current schedule and results and a list of Haifa's championships. With a history of Israeli football and links to other teams in Israel and beyond.

Israeli Soccer

http://www.sfu.ca/~kbutler/israel.htm

Soccer scores, up to the minute. Nothing but stats. You know, a lot of teams in the United States, in various sports, have nicknames like the "Chiefs," the "Redskins," and the "Braves," which some folks, notably Native Americans, find offensive. I have a solution: Rename all those teams after Jews. Wouldn't that be great? "And today, in NFL action, it's the Dallas Cowboys against the Washington Jews. And John Madden, those Jews are tough, aren't they?" "You got that right, Pat. Those Jews are tough, and boy do the fans love 'em."

Maccabi Elite Tel Aviv

http://www.cs.bgu.ac.il/~herouth/maccabi/

Fans of Israeli basketball can read all about Maccabi Elite Tel Aviv, the most successful basketball team in Israeli history. With links to an Israeli basketball mailing list you can join.

Moti Daniel

http://tltlinet.teletel.co.il/motid/index.htm

Meet Moti Daniel, star of the Israeli National Basketball team, at his website here. That's the difference between Israel and America. If he lived here, he'd have movie deals, rap albums, multigazillion-dollar deals. In Israel … he just gets a webpage. Actually, I'm sure he does just fine.

Soccer Rules!!!

http://t2.technion.ac.il/~c0453524/Soccer/menu.html

"Soccer rules!!!" reads the announcement at the top of this website, and by gosh, it sure does, right here. A mind-numbing array of game information, statistics, and opinion. Nirvana for the Israeli soccer fan.

Touch Football

http://www.jer1.co.il/media/atfi/

The Association of Touch Football in Israel proves that chess isn't the only Jewish contact sport. The website is pretty basic, but you can check out their schedule here.

Wingate Institute

http://www.orndorff.com/ijs/wingate.html

Israel's most prestigious institute for research and education in sports, phys ed, and sports medicine. The State of Israel has developed the Wingate Institute as a home for the "educational, professional, and scientific resources for the development of physical education, sport for all and sport as a means of social and physical rehabilitation." You can read short explanations of the various departments, which include a center for sports medicine, a school for coaches and instructors, the elite sports division (involving Olympic planning), and the International Jewish Sports Hall of Fame.

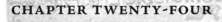

CHAPTER TWENTY-FOUR

ISRAEL—TRAVEL

THE WEB OFFERS a phenomenal approach to travel. You can find tours, photos, maps, fares, and information online. But, so far, few tour providers are taking serious advantage of the technology by offering on-line reservation services, travel updates, tours, and such. That's likely to change, of course, but here is the best of what I found available.

Coolest Clubs List

http://users-web.ort.org.il/~nsinger/clubs/index.html

All dressed up and nowhere to go? Not anymore, chum—not when there's "Israel's Coolest Clubs List," offering the discerning club-hopper maps, age ranges, drink prices, descriptions of the music scene, and recommended time to arrive. This list, maintained by 18-year-old Yiv Singer, offers you club listings organized by type of music, popularity, age range, and location. Voting for clubs is promised for the near future. Cool.

Cultural News and Events Gopher

gopher://israel.nysernet.org:70/11/israel/iis/cul

Cultural news and events in Israel at this site. Includes Hebrew writers, the Jerusalem 3000 festival's calendar of events, communications and media in Israel, and entire issues of the excellent publication *Panim*, which is produced by the Israel Ministry of Foreign Affairs and covers matters like publishing, music, and religion in Israel.

Eilat

http://www.eilat.com/

Eilat is the sun lover's vacation spot in Israel. Learn about your travel options here, where you'll find listings of and links to hotels, attractions, sports events, restaurants, and more. You can also view some pictures of Eilat.

Hotels and Travel

http://www.webscope.com/travel/israel.html

Links to hotel directories, chains, and kibbutzim. Lots of good stuff: maps, tourist information, events, national parks, how to find your way from Ben Gurion Airport, and a nice historical map of Jerusalem (click on Jerusalem Metro).

Intournet

http://www.intournet.co.il/

More links to various Israeli hotels, tours, and so on with Intournet, an online travel consultant. Site also links to some travel agencies. Useful, up to a point—the trouble is that a lot of travel information can be found much more easily in travel books; things don't change that radically in terms of hotels, restaurants, and tours. This could be a massive site—if they can find a way to get a lot more information than you can find in *Fodor's* or *Let's Go*. The list of travel agencies and tours is probably the high point.

Israeli Cities

http://www.ladpc.gov.il/citind.htm

Links to various Israeli cities and their home pages. A few of the major cities currently included are Jerusalem, Tel Aviv, Tiberias, Eilat, Haifa, and Ashkelon—there are a bunch more. For example, if you go to the Haifa Municipality home page, you'll find information about tourism, city history, social services, events, and business.

RECOMMENDED

Israeli Ministry of Tourism

http://www.infotour.co.il/

This site offers information about tourist destinations, hotels, restaurants, banks, sports centers, nightclubs, camping sites, and lots more related to tourism.

This website is really contrary to the way Israel works, which is usually characterized by chaos and utter disorganization. Part of the fun of being in Israel is asking six people for directions somewhere and getting twelve different answers, nine of which require knowledge of landmarks that for various reasons no longer exist: "Make a left where the Carmel Cinema used to be …"

A monster site and probably the best of the current travel sites because of its ease of use, organization, and completeness.

Kibbutz Beit Hashita

http://www.gilboa.co.il/

Kibbutz Beit Hashita, at the base of Mount Gilboa in Israel's Jezreel Valley, offers you an attractive and well-designed home page, describing everything from tourism to olive processing. If you've ever wondered what kibbutz life is like, click here. You'll learn a lot about how Israel's famed collective farms organize themselves, how they make a living, and how you can be a part of it. Not a "tour" in the traditional sense, but a pretty neat overview of a special Israeli way of life.

Rosh Hanikra

http://yaron.clever.net/nikra/nikra.htm

Photos and text on Rosh Hanikra, an ancient site in Israel featuring grottoes now reached by cable cars. This is basically a promotional site, geared to encouraging tourism, but you'll find some interesting reading here on the subjects of history and ecology.

Virtual Tour of Israel   RECOMMENDED

http://dapsas.weizmann.ac.il/bcd/bcd_parent/tour/tour.html

Includes photos, maps, and text—a super job from the Weizmann Institute. The historic map gives you a sense of how the territory of ancient Israel compares to the borders of Israel at various times in the 20th century. Click on Western Galilee and Carmel and you'll find a clickable map that offers insights into locations across the region. For example, did you know that Nahariya is known not only for its windsurfing and sailing but also for being the target of Katushka attacks from Lebanon? Maybe virtual travel is the safest way to go.

CHAPTER TWENTY-FIVE

KASHRUT, FOOD, AND DRINK

ARE YOU HUNGRY? These sites will connect you with Jewish and Israeli cuisine, recipes, and Jewish food from around the world. You'll find information about kosher food, kosher restaurants, and kosher supervision. Learn how to cook your favorite kosher Asian food and where to find kosher food in Austin, Texas. Learn about the foods you read about in the Bible.

> **NOTE**
> Our lawyers, those joyless people, asked us to remind you that we do not guarantee the hechsher, or kosher status, of any of the companies, services, or recipes provided herein; we list each site merely as a service to you.

Asian Kosher Recipes

http://www.kashrus.org/recipes/recipes.html

Craving Burmese Nga Tha Lauk Paung (soused fish)? Or some Sri Lankan Aioan Chua Noeung Phset Kretni (stir-fried chicken with mushrooms)? Dig into the kosher recipes from Singapore, China, and a host of other Asian countries. Learn about Asian cooking techniques and how to cook kosher Asian food. Learn which Asian ingredients are kosher and which ones to buy. Even read about Asian Jewish customs in articles about spending Shabbos in Japan, the Jews of Singapore, and a wide variety of South Asian Jewish communities. This fascinating and diverse site is sponsored by Asian American Kashrus Services. And remember, kosher chickens make excellent broth.

Austin, Texas, Jewish Food Page

http://www.zilker.net/~austinjc/jfood.htm

Where to find kosher food—traditional Jewish food—and even how to prepare for Pesach in Austin, Texas. Includes a link to the Chabad House of Austin.

Brooke Rose Vegetillas

http://www.webset.com/rose/

Kosher vegetable tortillas. Just like they made 'em in the old country.

California Cooks Kosher

http://www.w2.com/docs2/act/resources/jfs/jfs3.html

Sample recipes (and ordering information) from *California Cooks Kosher*. Mother's Spicy Mandelbread sounds good to me.

Cuisine, Laws, and Traditions

http://www.jcn18.com/food/

Recipes and explanations about Jewish laws and traditions related to food and holidays, written in a clear and concise manner by Philip Goldwasser, who knows and loves Judaism and Jewish cuisine. Matzo lasagna, *hamentashen* for Purim, and Shabbat Specials, like "Let's talk about kugels." This guy knows his way around a kosher kitchen.

Desert Rose Food Company

http://biz.rtd.com/desert_rose/

Certified kosher salsa and chips and other products from this Tucson-based food purveyor. Their page currently offers a gift pack containing a variety of types of kosher salsa. "Feel the heat and taste the passion," as the website promises; order via e-mail or get a catalog.

Foods of the Bible

http://www.ariga.com/tazine/biblfood/wheat.htm

Fascinating website explaining the foods mentioned in the Bible—with recipes, too. According to the Talmud, ancient Israel was renowned for the quality of the grains that grew there: barley, rye, oats, wheat, and spelt. Here you'll find intriguing and scholarly (yet fun) essays on the grains of the Bible—how they were grown, prepared, and served. And you'll find lots of recipes to make your table biblically correct. Highly recommended for cooks—and for eaters!

Glossary of Jewish Foods

http://www.healthtouch.com/level1/leaflets/5542/diet199.htm

Now you can finally understand what your grandmother was feeding you. Test yourself: Can you identify these three Jewish foods: farfel, gribenes, cholent? And what would your cardiologist think of your eating them? Recipes provided. A service of the American Dietetic Association. Not a searchable glossary, just a well-written list of definitions. Click on "Key Word Search" and type in **kosher**, and then go to "Kosher Jewish Food Glossary." You'll also find useful tips for eating healthy Jewish or kosher foods.

Gopher Menu of Israeli Cuisine

gopher://israel.nysernet.org:70/11/israel/iis/tour/recipe

The Israeli Embassy in Washington shows you that there really is an Israeli cuisine. You're thinking, what is it, 1,001 ways to serve tomatoes and cucumbers? Wrong. From their gopher menu to your family's table: everything from appetizers, soups, vegetables, and salads through main dishes, cakes, desserts, and beverages. *B'tai'avon.*

Gourmet and *Bon Appétit* Search Engine

http://www.epicurious.com/a_home/a00_home/home.html

The Big Search Engine That Could. Search *Gourmet* and *Bon Appétit* magazines by type of cuisine, ingredient, means of preparation, or any key word. Impressive. Numerous recipes for Jewish cuisine here.

Jewish Food

http://www.st-and.ac.uk/~www_sa/socs/jewish/food.html

A pleasantly written guide to the basics of Jewish food preparation; part of the *Bluffer's Guide to Judaism*, compiled by the Union of Jewish Students in the U.K. Emphasizes the biblical and rabbinical laws of kosher food preparation. You'll also find recipes for chicken soup, kneidlach, and lockshen—even an ode to chicken soup. I just like the idea of being able to visit the Chicken Soup Page. Makes me feel warm all over.

RECOMMENDED

The Jewish Holiday Kitchen

http://www.epicurious.com/

Ecstasy for fans of food expert Joan Nathan, author of several best-selling books on Jewish cooking. Holiday recipes excerpted from her books, with an option to e-mail yourself any recipe you like. How about a Hungarian Rosh Hashanah dinner? Are you desperate for a classic gefilte fish recipe? You'll find these and more here.

Jewish Recipes

http://www.eskimo.com/~jefffree/recipes/

This archive and mailing list, organized by Jeff Freedman, currently offers over 1,000 Jewish recipes, arranged by the first letter of their name and by Jewish holiday. This is truly a labor of love. Read the recipes here, add your own, or offer your comments regarding kashrut.

Kashrus Magazine

http://www.w2.com/kashrus.html

Kashrus magazine features articles on subjects like kosher chocolates and The Catering Game: their term for the fact that "many kosher caterers have no hashgacha" or kosher supervision. Their Consumer Alert warns of items that are not truly kosher. You'll find sample articles and subscription information here.

Kennedy Kosher Co-Op

http://www-leland.stanford.edu/group/kkc/

The Kennedy Kosher Co-Op offers kosher keepers in the Stanford/ Palo Alto, California, area a resource for shopping, and shows the rest of us how to organize a food co-op.

Knishes

http://www1.usa1.com/~knish/knish.html

Love and knishes—and mustard—from these Boston-based potato purveyors.

Kosher Coffee by Mail

http://tesla.directweb.com/cuppers/

Click here for kosher coffee. It's good to the last kleine bissel.

Kosher Eating in Chicago

http://condor.depaul.edu/~scohn/NTJC-Fd.html

If you're in Chicago, eat at these fine kosher restaurants and bakeries; a service kindly provided by the Niles Township Jewish Congregation in Skokie, Illinois.

Kosher Overseers of America

http://kosher.org/

This is the home page of the Kosher Overseers of America, Inc. If you have a product and you want kosher supervision, you might start here.

Kosher Restaurant Database

http://shamash.nysernet.org/kosher/krestquery.html

For the hungry kosher traveler. This database allows you to search by city or metropolitan area to find kosher restaurants. Listings include location, type of restaurant, and nature of *hashgacha* or rabbinical supervision. You can also add to the database kosher restaurants anywhere in the world. Currently most of the restaurants listed are in the U.S. and Canada. A thoughtful innovation from the Shamash Kosher Restaurant Team.

The Matzah Market

http://www.marketnet.com/mktnet/kosher/

If you have trouble finding kosher or Jewish foods in your local supermarket, you can order a wide variety here. You'll find kosher recipes at this website, too, along with links to other Jewish websites of interest.

Passover Charoset

http://swifty.dap.csiro.au/%7Ecameron/recipes/html/charoset.html

A recipe for *charoset*, the mixture of nuts, honey, apples, and wine that symbolizes the bricks and mortar the Jews used to build the pyramids of Egypt. My personal favorite at the Passover seder is the "Hillel sandwich," charoset and fresh horseradish on matzo. I'd love one of those right now, in fact.

The Reasoning and the Seasoning

http://www.halcyon.com/davidg/seasoning/

SaraBeth's Cream Cheese Brownies

- 1/4 cup butter (or unsalted margarine)
- 1/3 cup soft cream cheese (NOT the whipped kind)
- 1 cup sugar
- 2 beaten eggs
- 1/2 cup matzah cake flour
- 3 ounces bittersweet chocolate, melted & cooled
- 2 Tbsp. potato starch
- 1 cup finely chopped nuts

Cream butter, cream cheese. Add sugar and eggs, mix well. Stir in cake flour, potato starch, cooled chocolate, chopped nuts (reserving some nuts for the top). Spread batter in buttered 9x9 inch pan. Sprinkle reserved nuts over top. Bake at 325~ for 30 minutes. Cut into squares while warm.

Penina W. Freedenberg, Rockville, MD

Ordering information and sample recipes from *The Reasoning and the Seasoning*, a recipe book produced by the University Women of the University of Jerusalem in Los Angeles. You can try the recipes and then buy the book.

Recipes

http://www.marketnet.com/mktnet/kosher/recipes.html

Cyberkosher types from around the globe contribute their own recipes to this site; try some or post your own. You'll find recipes for SaraBeth's Cream Cheese Brownies, Chocolate Espresso Torte for Passover, Passover Cupcake Blintzes, and much more. Come back often, because the recipe base keeps growing. I'm getting hungry.

Wines in Israel

http://server.agmonet.co.il/~wine/

This home page, by Sasha Cooklin, offers a heady bouquet of information about wineries in Israel, wine weblinks, reviews, history, and wine facts. History of Israeli wineries, tourist information for each winery, and ratings of their offerings. Very imaginative and useful site with lots of neat information for oenophiles and alcoholics alike.

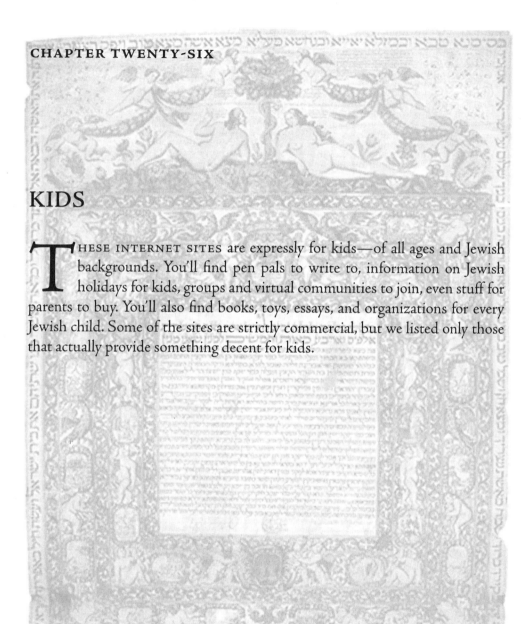

CHAPTER TWENTY-SIX

KIDS

T HESE INTERNET SITES are expressly for kids—of all ages and Jewish backgrounds. You'll find pen pals to write to, information on Jewish holidays for kids, groups and virtual communities to join, even stuff for parents to buy. You'll also find books, toys, essays, and organizations for every Jewish child. Some of the sites are strictly commercial, but we listed only those that actually provide something decent for kids.

Amsterdam Jewish Youth Community

http://www.ort.org/anjy/orgtions/holland.htm

Learn about the Amsterdam Jewish youth community at this text-only website.

ANJY Pen Pals

http://www.ort.org/anjy/penpals/penpals.htm

Use the Internet to find a Jewish pen pal anywhere in the world! Visit the ANJY Internet Pen Friend Service here. Either fill in a form or browse for pen pals. (Pen pals are sorted by age groups.)

Anne Frank Center USA   RECOMMENDED

http://www.annefrank.com/

Dedicated to the preservation of the famous Holocaust diarist's memory, the Anne Frank Center USA offers the story behind the diary, a visit to the secret chamber where Anne and her family lived, and much more. Jewish children for several generations have read Anne's diary, which provides a personal, quite harrowing, child's perspective on the war.

Bagelhead

http://www.gisd.com/bagelhead/

Kids, meet Bagelhead at his home page and make your parents buy his books for you! Bagelhead is a cartoon character who teaches Jewish values through stories and songs. You'll find excerpts of the songs and narration for very young children at the site. The stories take place on Jewish holidays; color sample pages can be viewed at the site, too.

Israeli Philharmonic Orchestra Youth Club

http://www.ipo.co.il/indexen.htm

Join the Israeli Philharmonic Orchestra Youth Club and learn about concerts and programs in Israel for children here. This could become a monster website, with musical excerpts, scores, discussions about music, and more.

Mendy and the Golem

http://www.nauticom.net/users/judaica/Mendy/MENDY.HTML

Follow the cartoon adventures of Mendy and the Golem, billed as "the world's only kosher comic book." Samples of the comics are available at this site.

A Network for Jewish Youth

http://www.ort.org/anjy/anjy.htm

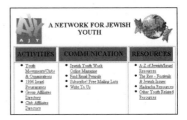

Offering events, travel, pen pals, mailing lists, and more to Jewish kids around the world. You can discover a whole world of new friends and things to do, and you can join the mailing lists and groups, too. Descriptions of each group, and information on how to become involved.

Noah Quiz

http://www.ualberta.ca/~yreshef/noahquiz.htm

Enter this contest and see how much you know about Noah and his ark. You'll find questions like "Who was the first drunk?" and "What sign does G-d make to remember not to bring a flood?" that will have students opening their Bibles. Prizes available only to Talmud Torah (Edmonton, Alberta) students, but take the quiz anyway.

Reference Bookshelf

http://www.shore.net/shalombk/ref.htm

An annotated bibliography (with hyperlinks) of books on Judaism for kids.

Tasmania Magazine

http://jumper.mcc.ac.uk/~tas/

Tasmania, Australia, presents the Talmud Appreciation Society, with back issues of *Tasmania*, their traditionally minded online magazine for kids. You'll also find a legal perspective on the week's Torah portion and information on local events, should you be passing through Tasmania any time soon.

Toys and More, for Sale

http://www.nauticom.net/users/judaica/jdckids.html

You can buy all sorts of toys, books, and videos at this site, from Bagelhead and Mendy and the Golem, to word games, Net pals, and more. "Net pals" are pen pals who communicate via e-mail; all kids can sign up and meet cyberfriends here.

Tu Bishvat, the New Year of the Trees

http://www.ualberta.ca/~yreshef/tuintro.htm

Learn about Tu Bishvat, the Jewish New Year of the Trees, and meet Honi Ha'Meagel, first-century B.C.E. Jewish scholar and, some say, miracle worker. A presentation of Dr. Nurit Reshef, of the Talmud Torah School, Edmonton, Alberta, Canada. An inspiration to others who want to use the Web to teach Judaism to children. You'll find out the whole story of Honi Ha'Meagel, and you'll learn a lot about Judaism.

Virtual Community for Jewish Children

http://www.cybergate.com/~printdr/vcomm.html

A California "CyberMom" has designed this web resource for you, to show you and your parents that there's a safe place for Jewish kids on the web. The author of the site intends to present a safe web chat room site for kids; keep visiting to see if it's up yet.

Waking in Jerusalem

http://www.iatech.com/books/waketoc.htm

Little ones and their parents will enjoy the Sharon Katz book *Waking in Jerusalem* at the City of Jerusalem home page. This is a sweet book; you'll find the entire text here as well as adorable pictures of street life in the Holy City.

CHAPTER TWENTY-SEVEN

LISTS, LINKS, AND DATABASES

THESE WEBSITES, which I call "link websites," offer long lists of links to Jewish Internet sites. The time it takes to put these together is enormous and it's clearly a labor of love, so prepare to meet a number of Heroes of the Jewish Internet.

Also, prepare to get lost for hours and hours and hours as you rocket back and forth among the countless websites, gopher menus, and other sites listed at each of these excellent lists. You can list your website, or your favorite website, with many of these lists as well. (Be sure to e-mail us at info@nostarch.com with sites that you'd like to see reviewed in the next edition of this book or that you'd like us to include on our website.)

The databases and search engines link you to libraries and collections around the United States, Israel, and the world. As always, type in URLs carefully, because even a one-letter mistake will make you miss your mark. But better yet, use the bookmark file on the disk that comes with this book to reach the websites that interest you.

Don't miss these lists: the A–Z of Jewish & Israel-Related Resources, the Ultimate Jewish/Israel Link Launcher, Shamash, the Jewish Archival Project, and Virtual Jerusalem. I review all of these, along with some other interesting sites, below.

A–Z of Jewish & Israel-Related Resources   RECOMMENDED

http://www.maven.co.il

Matthew Album, you are a true Hero of the Jewish Internet. An A to Z listing of countless websites. Happy browsing. Here you'll find a stunning number of Jewish-related links, with everything from "A Letter from Heaven" to WUJS Institution—a graduate center in Israel. The links are presented alphabetically and without annotation, so you'll spend a fair amount of time looking at things that may not interest you. But you can search by letter of the alphabet or by topic, and you can find virtually anything under the Jewish sun here. The list grows constantly; click on "New" and check out the latest sites Matthew Album has discovered for you. This list is an easy way to find the URL for any Jewish organization you can name.

ATARIM Search Engine

http://www.bestware.co.uk/atarim

You type in the word, and this search engine goes nuts finding corresponding Internet resources. It's good, but I'd start with the A–Z list (above)—it's a little faster and more comprehensive. If you want still more resources, this search engine will work well as a backup. I tried a couple of searches—Holocaust and Tiberias—and didn't turn up much that I hadn't found elsewhere. Seems like the search engines are all pretty much chasing the same Internet resources. Also, the searches can be slow—perhaps because the server for this engine is located in Israel. The provider, BestWare Ltd., is an Israeli software consulting and writing service.

Center for Computerized Research Services

http://www2.huji.ac.il/www_jcj/top.html

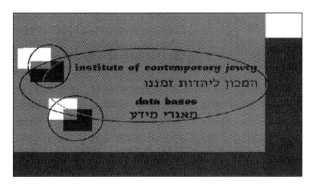

This Hebrew University project puts online for you the Center for Computerized Research Services, a database providing bibliographical information on everything you can think of related to 20th-century Jewish life. Already the database contains 30,000 entries. Search it from your home with Telnet. Included are the catalogs of the Oral History Division, the Steven Spielberg Jewish Film Archive and its Jewish Filmography Project, the Jewish Demography and Statistics Library, and the Vidal Sassoon International Center for the Study of Anti-Semitism.

I dropped in to the Spielberg Jewish Film Archive and found a fascinating essay on the role of film and video in capturing Jewish and Israeli history in this century. At this website, you can hire a freelance researcher in Israel to work for you or you can arrange to make use of the archives yourself. The entire Hebrew University website listed here is a fine tool for the researcher, academic, historian, sociologist, or film lover.

Hebrew University of Jerusalem

http://www1.huji.ac.il/

The home page of the Hebrew University of Jerusalem. Learn about the campus and connect to libraries and databases in Hebrew and English in and out of Israel. Serving about 30,000 visitors a month (so far), this website will speedily connect you to numerous departments—the computation center, various science and mathematics departments, the business and law schools, and various research projects. You do not have to be a Hebrew University student to take advantage of many of these databases, libraries, and services. Just drop on in.

Institute for Research of the Jewish Press   RECOMMENDED

http://www.tau.ac.il/journalism/

Potentially a very exciting site, this Tel Aviv University project (Institute for Research of the Jewish Press) will offer a database of 85,000 articles culled from the daily press and will also contain a historical archive with Jewish newspapers going back 300 years. A special section contains titles and details on 5,000 Jewish periodicals in some 40 languages published since the late 17th century, constituting only part of the estimated 15,000 Jewish periodicals thought to have existed.

The site is under construction and growing rapidly. You'll now find fascinating information on Jewish periodicals in Russia, information about publications, and links to other Jewish press-related sites.

Israel Sensitive Map

http://www.ac.il/israel_sens.html

If this worked, it would provide links to all the Web and gopher sites in Israel. Right now, you do get the map of Israel and on it a list of 15 clickable university and business websites, but, as of our last visit, none of the links worked.

RECOMMENDED

Jewish Feminist Resources

http://world.std.com/~alevin/jewishfeminist.html

Adina Levin has brought together in a concise and extremely useful manner information and weblinks on various subjects of interest to the Jewish feminist community. She organizes topics by major area and subgroups. Under Art you'll find Music, Stories & Verse, Visual Arts, and Film and Theater. Under Judaism, you can click on Bible and Midrash, Talmud and Halacha (Jewish Law), Holidays and Life Cycle, Spirituality and Theology, and Liturgy. Under each subhead you'll discover books, articles, weblinks, and other means of sharing ideas and knowledge. It's well worth your time.

Jewish Genealogy

http://ftp.cac.psu.edu/~saw/genealogy-jewish.html

This mailing list, for the discussion of Jewish genealogy, echoes the JewishGen group on FIDO net and the usenet newsgroup soc.genealogy.jewish. You'll also find links to many Jewish genealogy societies and Jewish history links from the American Jewish Historical Society to other web resources on Jewish history. These include the Borscht Belt/Catskills Institute, the Canadian Jewish Historical Society, the Dallas Jewish Historical Society, the Jewish War Veterans of the United States, and Tulane University's Holdings in Southern Jewish History. The Borscht Belt/Catskills Institute turns out to be the product of "a group of prominent Jewish scholars" who can rumba, play tennis, and juggle—but not at the same time.

Jewish Resources on the Internet

http://www.netaxs.com/~stessa/jewish.html

Part of the home page of Stessa Cohen, this page provides links to Jewish sites with a predominantly Jewish feminist, Philadelphian, and Reconstructionist/Renewal bent. Perhaps not surprisingly, her home page describes her as a member of a Reconstructionist congregation in Philadelphia.

Jewish Resources on the Internet (continued)

http://www.well.com/user/ari/jewish/jewish.online.resources

A list of online Jewish resources provided by Ari Davidow, the moderator of the WELL, a Sausalito, California, commercial computer conferencing service and one of the oldest forums on the Internet. Here you'll find a lengthy list of Jewish mailing lists on every topic in Judaism from *Aliyah in Science* newsletter through Yavneh North America. You'll also find mention of many of the sites we review for you in this book. Mostly of use for the list of mailing lists.

Jewish on the WELL

http://www.well.com/user/ari/jewish/jewish.html

A t this URL, the WELL provides a list of Jewish sites, virtually all of which you'll find reviewed in this book. This is also the home of the Jewish Conference, an annual online affair (I think) with discussions covering the Jewish holidays and customs, recipes, the situation in Israel, Jewish education, and Yiddish. The WELL dates back to the 1980s, before most of us knew anything about the Internet, and it's still growing.

Jewish/Israel History-Link Launcher RECOMMENDED

http://ucsu.colorado.edu/~jsu/history.html#geneal

Jewish history buffs, physicians, genealogists, and dedicated web-surfers will do backflips when they see this outstanding list of resources, part of the Ultimate Jewish/Israel Link Launcher (see below in this chapter), presented by the University of Colorado Jewish Student Union, true Heroes of the Jewish Internet. Many well-chosen links to extremely interesting websites. Sections include General Jewish History, Genealogy/Genetics/Disease, Ancient Israel, Diaspora History, and Israel History. For those interested in health matters such as Tay-Sachs, Gaucher diseases, Bloom syndrome, Neimann-Pick disease, and other health concerns of special importance to Jews, this list is the best place to go for related links. The best Jewish medical information on the Internet is right here.

Jewishnet RECOMMENDED

http://www.mofet.macam98.ac.il/~dovw/jw/l/mail4.html

A mother lode of mailing lists with Jewish themes. Organized neatly, alphabetically, attractively, and concisely. You'll find the name of the list owner, the subscription address, and a statement of purpose for each list, along with an extremely easy method of subscribing. For example, you'll find American Jewish Congress Action Alerts about legislative activities; Insights into Daf Yomi (a Talmud study plan allowing you to study one page of Talmud every day and complete the entire Talmud in seven years) from Ohr Samayach, a Jerusalem yeshiva; the Israeli Network for Social Responsibility; a Discussion of Hebrew Grammar and Etymology; and hundreds more.

Don't go overboard and subscribe to too many lists at once or your e-mail box will runneth over. A word to the cyberwise.

RECOMMENDED

The Judaica Archival Project

http://www.jer1.co.il/orgs/archival/bookintr.htm

Astunner. The Judaica Archival Project (JAP) is a nonprofit preservation and access program of Machon Mekorot Institute, located at the Jewish National and University Library on the Hebrew University Givat Ram campus in Jerusalem. Since 1990 they have preserved over half a million pages from thousands of rare, out-of-print, and classic Hebrew works in rabbinic studies. You can view their catalog online and order copies of extremely rare and out-of-print classic Jewish texts (both electronic and printed copies) including responsa, commentaries, rare first editions, kabbalah, encyclopedias, homiletics, incunabula, periodicals, Midrash, and basic texts in rabbinics from the world's largest Hebrew library. Their "Landmarks in Hebrew Printing" page offers an interesting history of Jewish publishing and "describes the unique role of printing in the transmission of Jewish traditions, highlights events in the history of Hebrew printing and the destruction of Hebrew books during persecutions."

Judaica and Jewish Links

http://phoenix.kent.edu/~dpowers/jewish.html

About twenty links to sites of Jewish interest, such as the U.S. Holocaust Museum and the Anne Frank Museum. It's useful, but it doesn't compare to such vast resources as the A–Z list mentioned above.

New York Public Library

http://www.nypl.org//research/chss/jws/jewish.html#coll

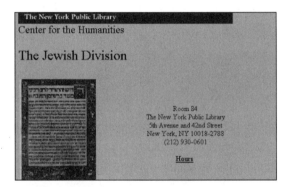

The New York Public Library offers a brief description of its Jewish Division's holdings here. The collection "offers commentary on all aspects of Jewish life" and also includes Hebrew- and Yiddish-language texts on general subjects. From the home page: "Here one finds a census in French of the Jews of Alsace taken in 1784 and a volume of essays written in German, examining eight hundred years of

Jewish life in Munich, as well as a Yiddish manual on stenography and a Hebrew text on aeronautics." The only thing it doesn't tell you is how you can gain access to these interesting things. If you go to http://www.nypl.org/ you'll be connected to CATNYP, the main search engine for the New York Public Library.

Palestinian Academic Network

http://www.planet.edu/

The Palestinian Academic Network, or PLANET, makes it easy to contact Palestinian academics and institutions. Its purpose is to provide scholars studying Palestinians with easy access to information, universities, and each other. Articles and many links to related home pages, such as the General Union of Palestine Students (U.K.) home page, the Palestinian Elections home page, and the "Jerusalem Water Undertaking."

Shamash

http://shamash.org/trb/judaism.html

The home of all things Jewish on the net. If it's out there, it's in here. Every topic from arts to websites to gopher menus. Extremely well organized and a model for anyone seeking to provide a central listing of information on the Internet. The Shamash page offers a clickable table of contents with every conceivable topic: Jewish Communities, Arts, Jewish Organizations, Products and Services, and FTP Archives are but a handful. These internal links take you to annotated external links, which is a propellerhead way of saying that if you click on the topic you're interested in, you'll find brief, helpful descriptions of and links to related websites and other Internet resources.

The Shamash project calls itself "The Jewish Internet Consortium," and rightly so—Jewish groups of every religious and political stripe are members and are linked here. Where else in the Jewish world can you find Peace Now and the Orthodox Union, Reform Judaism and Conservative Judaism, all under the same "roof"? Shamash, a product of the Board of Jewish Education of New York, is truly the place where the cyber-lion lies down with the cyber-lamb.

You'll also find texts of the Bible, commentaries, a kosher traveler's database, software, and mailing lists. This is simply not to be missed. Visiting the Jewish Internet without going to Shamash is like visiting Israel and skipping Jerusalem.

Synagogues Online

http://werple.mira.net.au/~aragorn/jew-syn.html

This page intends to provide links to congregations of all movements; currently there are just a few, but this could be an extremely large and useful resource. You'll find a longer list of links to shuls and congregations at Shamash, above.

RECOMMENDED
The Ultimate Jewish/Israel Link Launcher

http://ucsu.colorado.edu/~jsu/launcher.html

Nearly 5,000 links to everything Jewish on the Internet, from Hero of the Jewish Internet Steve Ruttenberg. Organized by topics: Politics, Judaism, Culture, Local, People, History, Anti-Semitism, Information, Travel, Business, Academic, and Organizations. Then organized by subheadings, with brief and useful annotations. Ruttenberg, a University of Colorado student, writes that he receives no funding (yet) from any Jewish organization. Hey, what he ought to do is forget grants and take this thing public!

Virtual Jerusalem

http://www.jer1.co.il/

This extensive site offers links to an ever-growing array of non-profit Jewish organizations. You can learn about everything from *aliyah* (emigrating to Israel), the arts, charity organizations, Holocaust studies, Zionism, and the Israeli government. There's a section on this week's Torah portion, radio programming and free I-Wave software with which to hear it, the latest news from Israel, and a Jerusalem photo album—all presented in an easy-to-use *USA Today*–style graphic display. Not to be missed.

Yellow Pages

http://www.dapey-assaf.com/

This search engine allows you to peruse the Dapey-Assaf Jewish Israeli Yellow Pages, covering the New York/New Jersey area, from the convenience of your laptop. They claim that over one million Hebrew-speaking people review their book each year. You can search their yellow pages as you would any printed yellow pages.

CHAPTER TWENTY-EIGHT

MUSIC

IF YOUR COMPUTER SUPPORTS MULTIMEDIA (if you're using a PC this means that you've got a sound card and speakers at a minimum), you can listen to real music through your computer. At first glance this may sound like having your television make toast. But the fact is that newer computer systems have phenomenal sound systems built in. The latest software for the Internet takes advantage of your computer's multimedia capabilities by delivering music (as sound files) through webpages and gopher and FTP sites. Music can easily be digitized so that it can be delivered through webpages. And with the proper browser on your end (like a recent version of Netscape Navigator or Microsoft's Internet Explorer), and any necessary plug-ins or helper applications, you should be able to download these sound files and hear them played through your computer's speaker. The result: Performers, groups, orchestras, klezmer ensembles, radio stations, and record companies can offer you sound samples of their wares. It really is pretty amazing.

When these sites offer music that you can listen to, you may need to have special software on your end. In most cases, the site itself will tell you what you need and will even offer a link to another site where you can download the necessary helper software. Sound software comes in a bunch of different flavors, but one of the most common is the RealAudio player (http://www.realaudio. com/products/player2.0.html). If a site says, for example, that RealAudio is required to listen to its music files, then you're not likely to be able to hear the music without the player. Dial into the site (like the RealAudio site listed above), download the program, and install it. If you have trouble getting these sound files to play on your computer or you can't get the software to install, you'll find helpful hints at the main, sponsoring site for the software.

I've divided the sites here into three sections: a general section (called "Tuning In Tunes"); sites focused on klezmer or Eastern European Jewish folk music; and a listing of performers.

Tuning In Tunes

Bob Dylan: Tangled Up in Jews

http://www.well.com/user/yudel/Dylan.html

What's up with folksinger Bob Dylan is the topic of this website. In author Larry Yudelson's own words: "This webpage is devoted to studying and collecting trivia relating to the Jewish religious/cultural odyssey of Shabtai Zisel ben Avraham, a.k.a. Bob Dylan." You'll find discussion about Dylan-lyrics to his music, links to other Dylan-related sites on the Internet, and even Hebrew translations of some of his songs. You'll also find parodies of Dylan's work, such as "I Dreamed I Saw Maimonides."

Chabad Classics

http://florida.com/chabadclassics/

Would you believe...easy listening classics of the Lubavitch Chasidim? This site brings you up to date on Chabad Classics' new and upcoming releases, providing previews and liner notes for each album. Chabad Classics is a series of easy listening music cassettes and CDs, capturing "the rich musical legacy of the Chabad Lubavitch Chasidim." According to the authors of the website, Chabad Classics "features the best in Chabad song and melody with performances by many prominent Jewish artists. From moving song of yearning to songs of soaring joy; from nostalgic tunes of Shabbos and Yom Tov to songs of deep reflection, Chabad Classics captures the essence of the mystical Jewish soul."

How important is music in Chasidic life? In the words of this website: "Song and melody occupy a prominent place in the Chasidic way of life. Since the essence of Chasidism lies in a denial of pessimism, melody is exalted as the means by which to dispel the gloom of despair and to replace it with the brightness of a joyful heart. The early leaders of Chasidism therefore either composed or encouraged others to compose sublime melodies. Over the years Chasidic songs have steadily increased in number. They have been handed down from generation to generation throughout the widespread Jewish community."

Israel Rock Guitar

http://www.siggroup.com/israel/ISRAEL~1.HTM

Israeli musicians and rock groups list themselves here; you can click on their song titles and either listen to their music or get chord charts for the songs. Featuring artists like David Broza, Gidi Gov, Shalom Hanoch, and Mashina. Listening to rock music over the Internet gives new meaning to the term "air guitar."

You can also list your own songs on the page.

Israeli Music

http://www.balladeer.com/cat/international/country/international5.html#isr

If you love Israeli music you can order hard-to-find recordings of a vast number of Israeli musicians at this website, sponsored by Balladeer Music. Incidentally, Balladeer offers vast collections of many different forms of international music; check them out for more than just their Israeli material.

Israeli Pop Chart

http://www.ctrl-c.liu.se/~dreamlover/anders/chart/israel/israel.html

Keep abreast of the top 20 pop singles in Israel here (and then you can order them from Balladeer Music, above). This pop chart could be a little more up to date; every time I went to check, the same chart, weeks or even months old, appeared. But maybe they've worked that out by now.

Israeli Pop Music: Radio Hazak

http://www.well.com/user/yudel/hazak.html

This is the website of Radio Hazak, a U.S.–based website sponsored by Larry Yudeson (Bob Dylan: Tangled Up in Jews, above). You'll find the latest news and commentary about Israeli music, lyrics for popular songs, listener polls, lists of important Israeli albums, links to popular Israeli bands and other Israeli music sites, and music samples.

"Jerusalem of Gold"

http://www1.huji.ac.il/jeru/song_of_jerusalem.html

Naomi Shemer wrote the song "Yerushalayim shel Zahav," or "Jerusalem of Gold" right at the time of the Six Day War in 1967. The song came out of nowhere but could be heard everywhere. I was nine years old at the time. My wonderful grandmother had gone to Israel and brought back a 45 of the song, which I played endlessly. I still get chills when I hear it. If you've never heard it, now's your chance. You can listen to "Jerusalem of Gold," in Real Audio, in its haunting entirety, at this webpage and hear a piece of Israeli history.

Jewish Music and Arts Information

http://www.columbia.edu/cu/jsu/web_page/jewpella.html

Now hear this: a fine resource with tons of links to Jewish music and arts pages. You can connect to any of several dozen groups like the Zamir Chorale of Boston, the Arbel Chorale of Philadelphia, or New York's a capella Beat'achon. You'll also find links to a Jewish Music List, and (as of this writing) four upcoming Jewish music festivals.

Jewish Music Gopher Menu

gopher://israel.nysernet.org:70/00/lists/jewish-music 921210

This gopher menu is the Internet at its most disorganized. If you want to go digging through a Jewish mailing list archive concerned with klezmer and other forms of Jewish music, try a few of the gopher files here. The problem is that the files are listed by date and without regard to content; nonetheless you can find some interesting information about little-known groups and recordings here.

Jewish World Music

http://www2.portal.ca/~jsiegel/about_jm.html#Preface

The history of Jewish music in a fascinating and well-written essay presented by the Jewish music group Tzimmes. This is an outstanding music-related website. You can download and play Tzimmes's music, and the essay about the history of Jewish music gives you a good reason to linger and get to know the group better. To learn more about Tzimmes, see the listing for their website below.

Kdam Eurovision

http://www.aquanet.co.il/web/kdam/

The Internet home of the Kdam Eurovision, or Pre-Eurovision Song Contest in Israel. This contest is a very big deal in Europe, and Israel has been participating since 1973. This is a very cool site. You can actually download all the songs that Israel has entered in this international competition, read about the songs and the artists, read music news, post your own opinions, and even vote for your all-time favorite Kdam Eurovision song. Perfect for homesick Israelis and also for Americans who want to enjoy Israeli pop culture. In RealAudio and Wave format.

National Jewish High School Choir

http://www.azc.com/client/sheri/hazamir/

Hazamir, the National Jewish High School Choir, travels to Israel to tour and sing. The group has outposts throughout the mid-Atlantic states and Boston. The site is fairly simple—you'll find a few paragraphs about the group and information about a winter festival in the New York area.

Radio 101 FM

http://www.jer1.co.il/media/web101/

The rock voice of Jerusalem, 101 FM. An attractively designed website tells you about the staff and programming of a new Jerusalem radio station; you can enter contests and dedicate songs to Jerusalemites.

Reshet Gimmel

http://teletel.co.il/gimmel/index.html

The home page of Israel radio's Reshet Gimmel, with news about the shows and the pop music it plays. With highly imaginative spelling. The station broadcasts in Hebrew, and it transliterates its program schedule into English for you here. If you click on "fun stuff," you get a "top 20 quiz" which will "let you place your vote and win many prizes." You can also listen to "sound tracks, jingles, and other cool stuff" and go "back stage" and read about the various on-air personalities.

SabraChat

http://www.irsociety.com/cgi-bin/webchat_doorway.cgi?Room=Israeli_Chat

SabraChat features chat rooms focused on Israeli social and cultural issues and events such as on-line interviews with Israeli recording industry types. If you click on the "Sabra Music Center" option on this home page, you'll find a selection of 30-second excerpts of Israeli songs recorded in Internet Wave file format; a 28.8 modem is suggested although a 14.4 will do in a pinch. You can find more Israeli chat venues in Chapter Seven of this book.

Klezmer

THE WORD "KLEZMER" is a Yiddish version of the Hebrew words "k'lay zemer," or musical instruments. Born in Eastern Europe, this Jewish folk music has caught on with American Jews in a very large way. You hear it at weddings, in concert halls, and on the radio. Now you can hear it over your computer, and you can certainly read all about it, here.

Ari Davidow's Klezmer Page

http://www.well.com/user/ari/klez/

News, reviews, vendors, and tons more, all about the world of klezmer, or traditional Eastern European Jewish music. You'll find the Klezmer Top Ten, contact information for "klezfolk" from Alaska to Italy, dozens of reviews and articles, information about the Chicago Klezfest (a three-day festival including klezmer), and links to many klezmer-related sites. True one-stop shopping for devotees of the klezmer lifestyle.

Austin Klezmorim

http://www.eden.com/~bamusic/

The Austin Klezmorim introduce you to Jewish folk music, Texas style, at this stylish webpage, offering information about the group, brief sound samples, and sheet music. The group describes itself as "a fusion of the old and the new, Eastern European, Middle Eastern and Oriental traditions fused with American Jazz from the 20's to the present, South American music, and Southwestern music."

David Perkins

http://www.cyberscribe.com:80/perkins/

Meet Jerusalem's King of Klezmer, the self-described "large guy with the red bushy beard," musician and instrument designer David Perkins. His site offers you samples of his music, information about klezmer in Israel, and just plain fun.

Mazeltones

http://www.seattle.wa.us/Mazletones

Meet the Mazeltones, Seattle's klezmer group, right here. In concert and on CD, the group offers a little of everything: music combining old Yiddish favorites, jazz, Broadway, and "an eclectic hot Israeli hora or two." They perform in English, Russian, Hebrew, and Yiddish. You can hear them, order their music, or even book them to perform via their website.

Performers

JEWISH AND ISRAELI MUSICIANS, composers, and groups of all stripes make use of the Internet to meet their fans, build awareness, offer samples, and sell tickets and recordings. You'll find rock stars, college a capella groups, orchestras, and klezmer ensembles. One of the hardest tasks musicians face is promotion. The Internet is an ideal tool for musicians and music lovers to find each other. How else could a small Texas klezmer ensemble make its music accessible to potential listeners, concertgoers, and CD buyers around the globe?

Arbel Chorale

http://users.aol.com/lipkinl/arbel.html

The basics about this Philadelphia-based young adult Jewish choir.

Dana Mase

http://www.j51.com/~mase/

Dana Mase describes herself as "a female Orthodox Jew and a singer and songwriter!" Why the exclamation point? Perhaps because singer-songwriter has never really been an acceptable job title for women in the Orthodox world, where tradition remains uncomfortable with the public performance of any woman's singing voice. She is certainly the first female Orthodox Jewish singer-songwriter I've ever encountered. Get to know the woman and her music here.

Debbie Friedman

http://www.jewishmusic.com/tara/dfr.htm

Debbie Friedman is one of the leaders in American Jewish spiritual music. Sample her songs here and learn more about her music.

Israel Philharmonic Orchestra

http://www.ipo.co.il/

This home page of the Israeli Philharmonic Orchestra includes the basics about the orchestra's conductors and history, and the current year's concert program listings.

Izhar Ashdot

http://shani.net/ashdot/

Izhar Ashdot, the Israeli singer, offers you sound samples, lyrics, and video at this site.

Jewish Collegiate A Capella Information

http://www.columbia.edu/cu/jsu/pizmon/jewpella.html

A listing, with links, of mostly northeastern Jewish collegiate a capella groups.

Magevet

http://pantheon.cis.yale.edu/~lizzz/magevet.html

Learn all about Magevet, Yale University's Hebrew a capella singing group "since 5753." You can even order their latest CD.

Piamenta

http://www.zstarr.com/piamenta/

Piamenta is Chasidic New Wave music. The *Village Voice* calls Yossi Piamenta the Chasidic Hendrix. Samples of their music, information, and more here. The *Voice* article calls Piamenta's music "wildly sprawling Arabic melodies spun up and away out of all visual relationship—screwed-tight Oriental outbursts punctuated by distant echoes of the electric-guitar pantheon, from Clapton to Zappa to Mahavishnu John." They rework traditional Chasidic melodies and cover rock songs as well.

Rabbi Rayzel Raphael

http://www.netaxs.com/~stessa/rabbi.html

Meet this Reconstructionist singer/songwriter/lecturer at her home page. She has written more than 60 new Jewish songs and prayers, including liturgy with themes of women in the Bible. She lectures on topics relating to Jewish spirituality and performs with two other women in a group called MiRaJ.

Shakshuka

http://ourworld.compuserve.com/homepages/Shakshuka/

Shakshuka is a Chicago-based trio of guitar, drums, and voice offering Sephardic and Israeli music with an alternative, jazz feel. Read about them and hear samples of their music here. ("Shakshuka" is also the name for a spicy eggs-and-tomato-sauce dish popular throughout the Middle East.)

Shlock Rock

http://www.jewishmusic.com/sro.htm

Shlock Rock keeps its fans satisfied, as 12 albums and two videos attest. The music offers Jewish identity, Jewish awareness, and Jewish pride. Lots of your favorite songs in "Stereophonic Shlock." They parody well-known rock songs and write Jewish songs as well in order to satisfy their growing legion of fans, known as "shlockers." They also perform about a hundred live concerts a year for "shlockers" around the globe.

Tzimmes

http://www2.portal.ca/~jsiegel/tzimmes.html

Tzimmes is a mostly Canadian group devoted to Jewish music. You can hear samples of their music and read about their members here. Click on Jewish World Music and find a valuable, Tzimmes-written introduction to the history of Jewish music.

The writing that accompanies the music on this website is so well done that it receives its own entry earlier in this chapter.

Zamir Chorale of Boston

http://www.zamir.org/

Visit this leading Jewish chorus at its website, where you can meet the members, check out their performance schedule, and order recordings and sheet music. You'll find online exhibits on Jewish music as well. At the time of our visit, the exhibit told of the choral music of the 17th-century Venetian Jewish composer Salamone Rossi. Text, sound, lyrics, and music to download. An interesting and wonderful service to Internet musicologists.

CHAPTER TWENTY-NINE

MYSTICISM AND KABBALAH

JEWISH INTEREST IN MYSTICISM dates back more than 2,000 years. The term "kabbalah," the study of mystical Jewish concepts, comes from the verb "to receive," implying that the knowledge is received one person at a time. Traditionally, kabbalah could be studied only by married men, age 40 or older, who had a "full belly" of traditional Talmud learning first. The World Wide Web is another step forward in democratizing the study of kabbalah and Jewish mysticism.

The sites in this section offer various sorts of introductions to kabbalah.

Adin Steinsaltz

http://www.glas.apc.org:80/~mali/english/kabbala/manifestation.html

Adin Steinsaltz is one of the great minds of the 20th century, in or out of Judaism. Read a lengthy excerpt from *The Thirteen Petalled Rose*, his beautiful book about Jewish mysticism, right here.

Gateway to Qabalah

http://www.webcom.com/~hermit/qabalah.html

A listing of resources on Jewish mysticism. All of a sudden white light poured out of my computer screen. Here you'll find annotated links to half a dozen kabbalah websites; brief descriptions of a small number of books on the topic; links to essays currently available on the Internet; and exercises "that will help you, in many ways." Intrigued, I clicked on the exercises link and found a relaxation method that looked good. It then offered to let me move on to the "Lesser Banishing Ritual of the Pentagram." I would have tried it, but I don't think I'm insured for it. Brought to you by Doug Evans.

Kabbalah Gopher Menu

gopher://infx.infor.com:4900/11.browse/**New%20Titles**/History/Jewish%20History--Diaspora

This gopher menu offers intriguing articles on the kabbalah, with references to Islamic, Christian, and Karaite approaches. Titles include "Muslim Writers on Judaism and the Hebrew Bible," "The Road to Redemption—the Jews of Yemen," and "Language and Culture in the Near East."

Kabbalistic WWW Pages

http://www.cyborganic.com/People/ovid/kbllinks.html

A lengthy list of kabbalistic resources on the Internet. Only a small number relate specifically to Judaism; indeed, until I visited this site I never knew that there existed Christian or Muslim kabbalistic traditions. You'll find an annotated bibliography of Lubavitch kabbalistic writing, a fascinating 18th-century study of kabbalah, and a large number of photographs.

Meru Foundation

http://www.shamash.org/judaica/meru/

The Meru Foundation, formed in 1983, sets forth the proposition that patterns can be detected in the way Hebrew letters appear in the text of Genesis. Esoteric but worth your time if you have a real bent for mystical thinking. This site is probably not for the newcomer to mysticism; you might want to get your feet wet elsewhere and then dive in here.

The 10 Sefirot of the Kabbalah   RECOMMENDED

http://www.ucalgary.ca/~elsegal/Sefirot/Sefirot.html#Map

An enjoyable, interactive introduction to kabbalistic thinking, from (no surprise) Hero of the Jewish Internet Eliezer Segal. You get a clickable "map" of the 10 "Sefirot," or divine emanations with which God created the world; click on the emanation you're interested in and receive a translation and description. Only Eliezer Segal could make the kabbalah this easy to understand. An excellent starting point for the seeker.

What Kabbalah Means to Me   RECOMMENDED

http://www.cyborganic.com/People/ovid/kbl.html

Kabbalah Now, a well-designed introduction to kabbalah with a bibliography and links to other kabbalah pages. You'll find many basic ideas of kabbalah described in a clear and understandable manner. Produced by a lover of Jewish mysticism, Ovid C. Jacob, who also lectures on the subject.

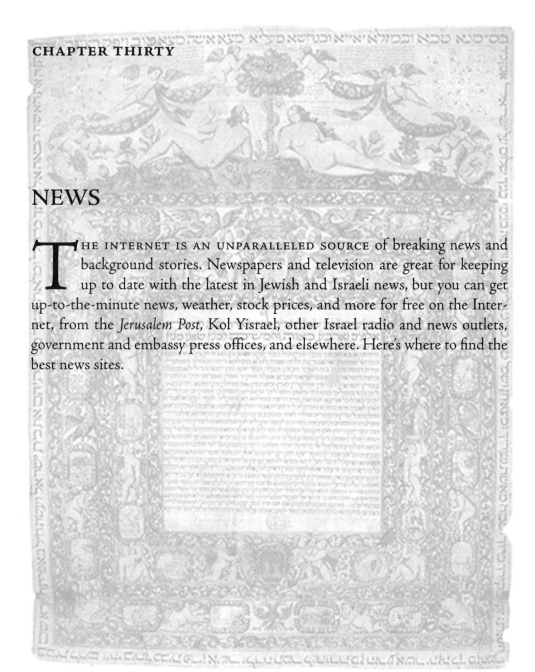

CHAPTER THIRTY

NEWS

THE INTERNET IS AN UNPARALLELED SOURCE of breaking news and background stories. Newspapers and television are great for keeping up to date with the latest in Jewish and Israeli news, but you can get up-to-the-minute news, weather, stock prices, and more for free on the Internet, from the *Jerusalem Post*, Kol Yisrael, other Israel radio and news outlets, government and embassy press offices, and elsewhere. Here's where to find the best news sites.

Artificia: Audio News from Israel RECOMMENDED

http://www.artificia.com/html/news.cgi

Kol Israel (Voice of Israel Radio) speaks through your computer in either English or Hebrew at the touch of a button. There are updated broadcasts several times throughout the day in RealAudio and Internet Wave format. There's also a chat room, Kol Israel's shortwave schedule in English and Hebrew, and help if you want to teach your computer to give you the news.

Arutz 7 RECOMMENDED

http://www.jer1.co.il/media/arutz7

Arutz 7 is Israel's only independent radio station. Its valuable webpage presents today's news and opinion in a fairly unbiased manner, a digest of Arab press news (from a conservative, Jewish perspective), "Good News from Israel" (a nice change of pace), and even news broadcasts as sound files—although they were only available in Hebrew the last time we checked. You'll also find an e-mail news service to subscribe to. An excellent source of information for what's going on in Israel and for the political and legal stories that don't make the world press.

A. Engler's Jewish News Links

http://www.libertynet.org/~anderson/newslist.html

Links to lots of Jewish news outlets, prepared by A. Engler Anderson of Philadelphia, Pennsylvania. Although this isn't a fancy site—and it's clearly made up of what Mr. Anderson finds interesting (and why not? It's his site!)—you'll find lots of useful links here. You'll also find his "Unofficial Jewish Print News Media List," a great way to promote your Jewish-oriented product.

RECOMMENDED   ## Israel On Line

http://www.haaretz.co.il/top.html

Israelis and Hebrew speakers can benefit from IOL, or Israel On Line, a service of the Israeli daily Hebrew newspaper *Haaretz*. A big, impressive site with lots of information in Hebrew; you'll need software and fluency in Hebrew in order to put it together.

Israeline

http://gauss.technion.ac.il/israeline/

You'll find a daily summary of news from the Israeli press together with several years' worth of archives here. Israeline is a great resource, especially if your hometown paper gives Israel just a passing mention. And you can even subscribe to the Israeline mailing list: Send e-mail to listserv@pankow.inter.net.il with the following in the message body

SUBSCRIBE ISRAELINE *your name*

You'll receive an acknowledgment and information file in return.

Jerusalem Post   RECOMMENDED

http://www.jpost.co.il/index.html

If you like the *Jerusalem Post*, you'll love this website, which boasts a comprehensive edition of the day's *Post* delivered to your cyber-doorstep. You'll find just about everything you'd find in the regular newspaper—news, business, opinion, columns, features, sports, entertainment, weather, real estate, stocks, companies in the news, and more. And, unlike the printed newspaper, you'll find links to interesting and related sites on the Internet, where you can dig even deeper into the issues that interest you. Their page is attractive, informative, and easy to search—the next best thing to being there.

Jerusalem Report   RECOMMENDED

http://www.virtual.co.il/news/news/j_report/

Read selected stories from the current and past issues of *Jerusalem Report*. You can also subscribe and have the full print version sent to your home. An excellent way to stay on top of the Israel scene and current Mideast events. Published bi-weekly, the *Jerusalem Report* is most comparable to *U.S. News and World Report* or the *Economist* and provides analysis of the controversial issues facing Israel today—whether they're occurring in Israel, the Middle East, or the corridors of power in Washington.

RECOMMENDED

Jewish Communications Network

http://www.jcn18.com/news/

Bookmark this baby and you'll get daily news updates from every source imaginable: CNN, the *New York Times*, Reuters, Voice of America, the *Times of London*, and more. You'll also find links to many of the other news sources listed in this section of *The Guide to the Jewish Internet*, including the *Jerusalem Post* and the *Jerusalem Report*. The discussion forums are great.

RECOMMENDED

Jewish Post

http://www.jewishpost.com/jpnews.html

New York's *Jewish Post* online is everything an online Jewish newspaper should be: well written, rich in information, and a source of complete articles. This is well worth your bookmark and a fine companion to other Israeli news sources, because this one focuses as much on U.S. Jewish affairs as on Israeli matters.

Jewish Review

http://www.teleport.com/~jreview/

This Oregon newspaper, the "first Jewish newspaper on the Internet," offers news and features. If you're from Oregon, it's well worth your time; if not, you might try the larger sources first.

News About Israel

http://www.xs4all.nl/~ambisra/press/press.htm

Includes wrap-ups of news from today's editions of Israeli news-papers coming to you from the Israeli Embassy in Holland. Nicely organized with stories, Israeli government briefings, a news archive, policy statements by Israeli officials, and subscription information for the Israel Information News by e-mail.

News in Hebrew

http://www6.snunit.k12.il/hebrew_news/manchi_hebrew_news.html

News in Hebrew, updated daily, from the Hebrew University in Jerusalem; you need Hebrew fonts for this website.

Shomron News Service

http://www.borealis.com/sns

Names are everything in Israel. "Shomron" is the Hebrew name for the Samaria region of the West Bank. Those who refer to the West Bank as Yehuda (Judea) and Shomron are generally supportive of the right-wing or Likud position with regard to the peace process. The Shomron News Service was set up in 1994 to provide "accurate and detailed information" about the peace process. We cannot vouch for accuracy but we can make a pretty safe guess that it's pro-settler. News, archives, links, and the intriguing "Middle East Playing Cards," which, alas, were unavailable at the time of our visit.

Tel Aviv Stock Exchange

http://www.tase.co.il/

Closing stock prices from the Tel Aviv Stock Exchange, business information, business links. Also an eight-minute audio tour of the stock exchange; publications including lists of companies, mutual funds, and futures trading; and free files offering stock and bond data.

Voice of America

gopher://gopher.VOA.GOV/11/newswire

News about Israel—and the rest of the world—from the Voice of America. Cool site, because it provides tons of interesting news and features from a respected news source.

Weather in Israel

http://www.intellicast.com/weather/jrs/

Is it raining in Jerusalem? The four-day forecast is yours if you click here. Worldwide weather, too. I love this stuff.

CHAPTER THIRTY-ONE

ORGANIZATIONS

A LONG, LONG TIME AGO in Jewish history, say, about 1993 or earlier, if you wanted to find out about a Jewish organization, you had to track down the group in the phone book, call a reference librarian, or do some other time-consuming activity. The Internet, of course, changes everything. Jewish organizations related to social service work, politics, science, diplomacy, security issues, Jews in prisons and jails, history, education, medicine, and even adoption all have locations on the Internet for you to visit. You'll find the purpose of the group, background information, news, related sites, and ways to become involved.

This section lists a variety of Jewish organizations in the United States and Israel that cover a wide range of topics. If you are involved in a Jewish organization that hasn't gone online yet, you can study similar groups' websites and get some ideas. For the websurfer, it's free information, easily obtained. For the organizations, it's a chance to spread the message, find new members, or solicit financial support. Everybody wins.

Aleph Institute

http://www.shamash.org/judaica/aleph/

A fascinating website. The Aleph Institute assists Jews in American prisons and jails in many ways. Aleph provides literature about Judaism and Jewish ritual objects like talleisim and tefillin; arranges visits from rabbis and rabbinical students; works with the prison system to ensure fair treatment for Jewish worship; and more.

In the "Shemoneh Esreh," or traditional 18 Blessings" prayer, Jews traditionally refer to God as "the freer of captives." Maintaining contact with Jewish prisoners and obtaining, where possible, their release is an important aspect of traditional Judaism. Learn about an organization dedicated to this vital purpose.

AMCHA

http://www.jer1.co.il/orgs/amcha/amcha1.htm

A charitable organization offering support to Holocaust survivors and their families. Read their newsletters and annual reports here. You can read about the various regional branches of AMCHA and learn about the social and psychological services they provide their clientele.

America-Israel Political Action Committee

http://www.aipac.org/

The America-Israel Political Action Committee (AIPAC) is the leading voice for Jewish affairs in Washington and in state governments across the country. Learn what AIPAC does and how you can become involved in the political process as it affects American-Jewish relations and U.S. policy in the Middle East.

American Jewish Historical Society

http://challenge.tiac.net/users/ajhs/index.html

This organization, founded in 1892, offers an overview of its publications, archival holdings, and museum at this website. Of particular interest: a bibliography of works on American Jewish history and a listing of related websites. Click on Essential Readings and you'll find the bibliography, which will get any researcher started on a wealth of information about Judaism.

Anti-Defamation League

RECOMMENDED

http://www.adl.org/

The Anti-Defamation League (ADL) fights anti-Semitism through programs and services that counteract hatred, prejudice, and bigotry. Visit their site, jammed with vital, up-to-the-minute information about anti-Semitism in the U.S., on campus, and worldwide. You'll find recent issues of *ADL on the Frontline*, a periodic newsletter of ADL. You can also select, by topic of your choice, ADL focus papers—timely information on ADL activity by subject—press releases, and report summaries. Virtually all of the categories I visited, such as affirmative action, anti-Semitism-USA, civil rights/Supreme Court, all had been updated within the previous week. This is using the capabilities of the Internet to the maximum—free and easy distribution of timely and important information. A stellar site.

B'nai Akiva

http://www.jer1.co.il/orgs/akiva/ak.html

A short website providing background on this pioneering Zionist youth movement. Activities and information on how to join or support B'nai Akiva. I would be fascinated to read material from B'nai Akiva's archives at their site; the group's roots sink deep into early Israeli history and settlements in Jewish Palestine.

B'nai B'rith

http://bnaibrith.org

Welcome to
B'NAI B'RITH
INTER⚡CTIVE

"על שלשה דברים העולם עומד:
על התורה ועל העבודה ועל גמילות חסדים"
"The world rests on three foundations:
study, service, and benevolence."
ETHICS OF THE FATHERS

This is the home page of the international Jewish service organization, B'nai B'rith. Of particular interest: the 100-year index of *Jewish Monthly*, the B'nai Brith's publication, and an elegantly organized Jewish calendar that will take you into the next century. The Political Action Update provides important analysis of Capital Hill issues affecting U.S.-Israel relations, welfare reform, and anti-terrorism legislation. You'll also find upcoming events, the week's news releases, and job openings.

Board of Jewish Education

http://shamash.nysernet.org/bjeny/

An all-too-brief overview (roughly a page of text at our more recent visit) of this leading Jewish educational services provider. The Board of Jewish Education of New York meets the educational needs of the Jewish community by providing teachers, training, support, curriculum advice, and much more, to schools, school boards, and parents.

Coalition of American Jewish Educators

http://shamash.nysernet.org/caje/

The Coalition of American Jewish Educators brings together all those interested in Jewish education. Their last conference attracted 2,200, and their home page offers information about the organization as well as a list of their publications.

Congress of Secular Jewish Organizations

http://www.netaxs.com/~csjo/csjo.html

The Congress of Secular Jewish Organizations is an umbrella group for Jewish groups, mostly in the U.S. and Canada, focusing on the political, social, ethical, and cultural aspects of Judaism. They focus on those parts of Judaism outside the framework of organized religion, and offer study opportunities with regard to tradition, history, literature, music, art, languages, Yiddish, and Hebrew. You'll find links to many of their member groups, schools, and congregations at this website. Their Publications section offers books that describe secular observances of Jewish holidays like the Jewish New Year and Passover, as well as Yiddish stories translated into English.

Freeman Center for Strategic Studies

http://freeman.io.com

The purpose of the Freeman Center for Strategic Studies is "to improve Israel's ability to survive in a hostile world." The Center does research on military and political issues and has a decidedly Likud bent. This Texas-based think tank offers at its website articles and interviews focused on Israel's security issues. You can read the *Maccabean-Online* for political analysis and commentary on Israeli and Jewish affairs. Articles include "Arafat's Secret Plans for 'The Total Collapse of Israel,'" "The Great PLO Takeover," and "Understanding Israel's Islamic Terrorist Enemies: Some Serious Reflections." A useful resource for those who want a broader background on security issues; you can also order related books here.

RECOMMENDED

Hadassah

http://www.hadassays.org.il/

Hadassah, the largest women's Zionist organization in the world, offers education and counseling services to young people in Israel. Read about them and find links to other Hadassah websites here. With internal links to the Hadassah College of Technology, the Hadassah Career Counseling Institute, and the Hadassah Youth Center.

Institute for Jewish Medical Ethics

http://www.hia.com/hia/medethic/

This San Francisco–based medical organization sponsors conferences on Jewish medical ethics. They seek to identify underlying principles of Jewish law, as found in the Bible, Talmud, and other works; relate these principles to the practice of medicine; and review recent developments in areas like AIDS research and genetic screening. Read about the Institute and its programs here.

International Coalition for Missing Israeli Soldiers

http://www.cyberscribe.com/mia/

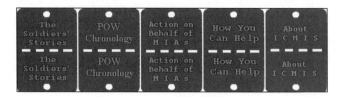

The International Coalition for Missing Israeli Soldiers seeks the return of six Israeli soldiers who have been captured since 1982 and are presumably being held in Syria or Iran. The website hosts the soldiers' stories, a time line of relevant events, and information on what you can do to help.

JACS: Jews in Recovery from Alcoholism and Drug Abuse

http://www.shamash.org/health/jacs/

Denial isn't a river in Egypt. Contrary to myth, Jews are just as susceptible to alcoholism and drug addiction as anyone else. JACS is an international organization supporting Jews in recovery.

Visit this site for *Grapezine*, JACS's online recovery magazine. You'll find an online "meeting," comments from rabbis, information on retreats, cartoons on Jewish denial, and much more.

Jewish Adoption Information Exchange

http://www2.webassist.com/stars-of-david/index.html

This website provides a wealth of information on Stars of David International and other resources for Jewish families concerned with adoption. You'll find links to a range of Jewish adoption resources online (newsgroups and mailing lists as well as other webpages), thoughtful articles and stories about adoption, and membership information.

Jewish Defense League

http://www.jdl.org/

Home page of the Jewish Defense League, perhaps the most controversial of all Jewish groups, founded by the late Rabbi Meir Kahane in 1968. Information on Israeli politics, U.S. Jewish-Christian relations, Nazism on the Internet, and the "Five Principles of the Jewish Defense League," the group's philosophy and statement of principles.

Jewish Social Justice Network

http://shamash.org/hc/jsjn/index.html

The Jewish Social Justice Network, brainchild of magazine editor and author Leonard Fein, supports "tikkun olam"—the concept of mending the world through social justice. Learn about this new group here. With connections to other social justice websites including the Jewish Social Justice Network Electronic Chavura.

Jews for Racial and Economic Justice

http://www.columbia.edu/~ljw17/jfrej/

Jews for Racial and Economic Justice, founded in New York City in 1990, offers educational programming, community organizing, and bulletin excerpts at its home page. This progressive group works for social justice among the various ethnic and racial groups that call New York home.

Jews in Prison   RECOMMENDED

http://www.sbchabad.org/sbchabad/prison/

Jews in Prison is a project of Chabad of Santa Barbara, California. The author, a rabbi, has visited Jews in prisons and jails across the United States for the past 15 years and offers a sensitive, well-written, and fascinating guide for Jewish inmates and their families. Intriguing and eye-opening.

Joint Distribution Committee

http://www.ort.org/communit/jdc/home.htm

Relief, rescue, and reconstruction: The Joint Distribution Committee (JDC) has been providing emergency services to Jews for 80 years. The organization was initially founded as a short-term means of aiding Jews affected by World War I, but as the troubles of European Jewry increased, the U.S.-based JDC remained in business. Get the basics about the JDC at this rapidly growing website. You can read, for example, about their current efforts in the former Soviet Union, which include helping Jews learn about their heritage and helping Jewish communities in Asia. (And leave the "y" off "community" in the address to avoid becoming lost in cyberspace.)

Knights of Jerusalem

http://www.erols.com/harari/koj/kojindex.html

Why are these knights different from all other knights? Because they're the Knights of Jerusalem, a pleasant, loopy, dare I say quixotic, group, whose goals are, um, I'm not sure. But they sound nice enough. Jewish Knights? Here's what their FAQ tells me: "The order was founded by two brothers, Nathaniel David Harari and Yasha Manuel Harari, in the state of Israel, in the year 5752, according to the Hebrew calendar. The order has traditional support, but maintains independence from such protocol and precedence. Instead, the order has replaced traditional ordaining with a vibrant, open, and forward-thinking vision of what knightly orders ought to strive for, including a just world and a good way of life." Does that answer your question? It sounds more like a 12-step group for Jews addicted to chess. But what do I know. Read about them and their members here.

Mahane Nefesh Bri'ah

http://www.ix.co.il/mnb/mnb.htm

Mahane Nefesh Bri'ah (MNB) offers Ethiopian, Russian, Israeli, and physically challenged children programs and services. Get to know their work here. You'll find the after-school program, the visitors museum, and the MNB summer camp all described here. Obviously, one of the greatest challenges of any social service program is to get the word out. This website can serve to inspire other social service groups to use the Internet to make contact with possible supporters.

Mosaic   RECOMMENDED

http://wymple.gs.net/~myron/mosaic.html

Jews hiking. Jews camping. A Socialist utopia from the 1890s? No—it's Mosaic. Mosaic is the name of a system of Jewish outdoor clubs (chapters) in many cities in the U.S. as well as in Canada and Israel. Put down your mouse, turn off your computer, and get outside with the members of Mosaic. You can meet them by visiting the website and finding the chapter nearest you; e-mail links mean no muss, no fuss.

A recent Mosaic trip included scuba diving and eco-adventuring in the Netherlands Antilles. Prices are reasonable, and it beats the hell out of another singles weekend in the Catskills.

National Jewish Committee on Scouting

http://shamash.nysernet.org/scouts/

The National Jewish Committee on Scouting promotes Jewish involvement in the Boy Scouts movement. Find out how they do it, where to find Jewish-sponsored scouts units, follow links to other scouting resources on the Internet, even subscribe to the J-Scouts mailing list.

I'd like to see them get busy on Kosher Boy Scout Cookies, but that's just one man's opinion. Hmm. Mitzvah Mints?

National Jewish Democratic Council

http://www.webcom.com/~digitals/njdc/

This group, founded in 1990, seeks to build upon the traditional connections between Jews and the Democratic party. You can browse their articles and press releases here, as well as learn how to get involved.

ORT

gopher://ortnet.ort.org:70/11/About%20ORT

ORT is one of the world's largest and oldest technical training institutions. We associate it in our minds with the State of Israel, but ORT actually was founded back in 1880 in St. Petersburg, Russia, and currently has programs all over the world. You can get absolutely everything ORT at this gopher menu, including history, present activities, skills taught, and statistics.

Social Service Organizations

gopher://israel.nysernet.org:70/11/ajfca

Dragnet-style "just the facts" about a phenomenally large number of Jewish social service organizations, by gopher and by state and Canadian province. One might have wished for a little more information about each listing, perhaps.

U.S.–Israel Biotechnology Council

http://www.usibc.org/

Learn about biotechnology in Israel at the website of the United States–Israel Biotechnology Council. You'll find an extremely useful overview of Israel's biotech industry as well as information about the "Alliance" conference, which the Council sponsors, bringing together U.S. and Israeli biotech and related firms.

Wolk Center for the Jewish Deaf

http://www.infoshop.com/wolkcenter/

The Wolk Center for the Jewish Deaf is designed to allow Jewish deaf students "to become familiar with and express their identity as Jews." With links to Jewish and deaf sites. You can subscribe to the deaf Jewish students e-mail list by sending e-mail to listproc@infoshop.com. Leave the subject line blank. The first and only line of the message should read:

subscribe DeafJewishList *yourname*

World Jewish Congress

http://www.jer1.co.il/orgs/wjc/intr.htm

A supremely informative website. The World Jewish Congress (WJC) refers to itself as the "representative roof body of Jewish communities across the globe." An advocate for Jewish interests worldwide since 1936, the WJC offers you fascinating and timely updates on Jewish politics and policies affecting Jews everywhere. You'll find global Jewish updates—monthly digests of news directly related to Jewish communities around the world; policy dispatches—brief and timely analyses of issues of immediate concern; policy forum—in-depth examinations of current topics by noted authorities and researchers; policy studies—comprehensive examinations of topics in Jewish affairs; *Gesher*—a Hebrew-language journal of Jewish affairs featuring analytical essays and book reviews; and *Dialogues*—a twice-yearly interfaith newsletter. This site is rich in valuable information, and the best part is that it's all free, whenever you want it. Check it out regularly.

World Zionist Organization

gopher://shamash.nysernet.org/hh/wzo/

This gopher menu offers educators information about trips to and study of Israel—study "modules" on everything from Jewish heritage to missing Israeli prisoners of war. The only trouble is the method of organization—it's about as tidy as my top dresser drawer. If you root around, you will find useful things, though one might wish for clearer headings.

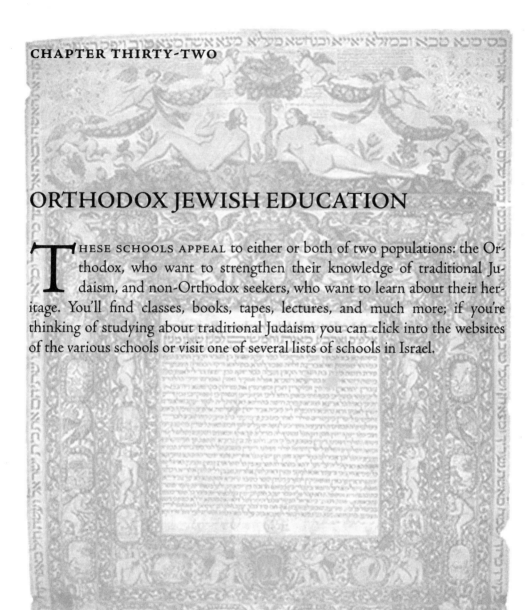

CHAPTER THIRTY-TWO

ORTHODOX JEWISH EDUCATION

THESE SCHOOLS APPEAL to either or both of two populations: the Orthodox, who want to strengthen their knowledge of traditional Judaism, and non-Orthodox seekers, who want to learn about their heritage. You'll find classes, books, tapes, lectures, and much more; if you're thinking of studying about traditional Judaism you can click into the websites of the various schools or visit one of several lists of schools in Israel.

Aish HaTorah

RECOMMENDED

http://www.catalog.com/aish/index.htm#Menu

Aish HaTorah opened its doors in Jerusalem in 1974 to attract Jews on their spiritual quests and help them find their spiritual and intellectual Jewish roots. The school has burgeoned over the past two decades into a major, international force in Jewish learning.

Its home page offers information about its courses in Jerusalem and around the world. You can also download lectures on traditional Judaism for no charge; a gift shop offers tapes, books, and other items. The lectures are superb and well worth your time.

Jerusalem One

http://www.virtual.co.il/education/education/6.htm

A resource listing yeshivot, seminaries, and other educational institutions in Israel, with hyperlinks. An ambitious project to bring under one cyberroof all the educational possibilities in the Holy Land. If you're thinking of going to Israel to study anything at all, start here.

Michlalah

http://www.jercol.macam98.ac.il/

The basics about this school for Jewish women in Jerusalem. The page was under construction at the times of our two visits. They offer online classes for free; the focus appears to be on computer technology.

Midreshet Lindenbaum

http://www.jer1.co.il/orgs/yeshiva/ohrtorah/midresh.htm

A yeshiva for women, dedicated to providing the same quality Talmudic education that men traditionally have received. Located in Jerusalem. Learn the basics about them here.

Midreshet Rachel

http://www.torah.org/programs/noam/pages/mrhome.htm

Midreshet Rachel was founded in 1983 in response to the demand of a group of college-educated Jewish women who wanted to explore their identity as women and as Jews using classical Jewish texts. Approximately 40 women, mostly from outside Israel, attend the school, located in Jerusalem's Givat Shaul neighborhood. The website offers a brief introduction to the school and its offerings.

Neve Yerushalayim College

http://www.shamash.org/judaica/neve/

An Orthodox yeshiva for Jewish women of all Jewish backgrounds—or none. An opportunity to learn about traditional Jewish belief and practice; year-long programs and summer learning programs as well. Neve, founded in 1970, is the women's branch of Ohr Samayach; see the next entry, just below.

Ohr Samayach Jewish Learning Exchange   RECOMMENDED

http://www.jer1.co.il/orgs/ohr/web/jle/index.html

One of the oldest and largest *baal teshuva yeshivot* or schools specializing in the needs of secular Jewish men who want to learn about traditional Judaism. Ohr Samayach now offers classes at sites around the world, from Jerusalem to Russia, from Los Angeles to Gibraltar. Their website is packed with information about their programs in Israel and around the world. The related program for women is Neve Yerushalayim (see previous entry).

Orchos Chaim

http://www.shamash.org/judaica/orchos/

Orchos Chaim is a small yeshiva in Jerusalem for men. You can read testimonials and course descriptions at this website.

Yeshivat HaMivtar

http://www.jer1.co.il/orgs/yeshiva/ohrtorah/hamiv.htm

A yeshiva for Jews from secular and Orthodox homes. Founded by Rabbi Chaim Brovender in Jerusalem; now in Efrat, 20 miles south of Jerusalem. This attractive, if brief, website provides information about the new campus, the student body, the faculty, and the course catalog; there's also a *Chanukah* magazine. The yeshiva is for men only but has a women's division where the women study the same texts, and in the same manner and with the same instructors, as the men.

Yeshivat Kiryat Arba

gopher://gopher.jer1.co.il:70/11/relig/arba

Now here's a super way to shake up your parents: Tell them you're off to study Talmud at Yeshivat Kiryat Arba, just outside Hebron.

This yeshiva is part of the "hesder" system, under which Israeli young men serve five years in the Israeli army in all-Orthodox units, interspersing yeshiva study with their military service. Kiryat Arba is near the location of the biblical tomb of Machpelah, the traditional resting place of Abraham and Sarah. This gopher menu offers an essay on the yeshiva and its relationship to the Israeli Defense Force (IDF); articles by the Rosh Yeshiva, or Dean, Rabbi Eliezer Waldman; and *A Voice from Hebron*, the English-language publication of the yeshiva.

Yeshivot in Israel

http://www.rpi.edu/~mandes/

A remarkable webpage, if only for the variety of yeshivot, or Jewish Talmudical academies, represented. Click on Highlights in Jewish Thought and you'll be brought to a menu listing educational resources from a large number of Israel-based English-speaking yeshivot. Usually these schools keep their own material on their own pages, but here everyone seems to get along. Especially worthy of note: essays by Dr. David Gottlieb of Ohr Samayach on the "Truth of the Torah," in the TORAH: The Permanent Connection link.

CHAPTER THIRTY-THREE

ORTHODOXY

ORTHODOX JUDAISM IS REPRESENTED on the Internet in far greater proportion than its numbers might suggest. This makes perfect sense: Orthodoxy thrives on information, commentary, and the dissemination of texts—and all those things are easily accomplished on the Internet. This section is not just for Orthodox Jews. Any Jew with an interest in traditional learning will find plenty to see here—readings, lectures, discussions, explanations of the weekly Torah portion. Key sites not to be missed: Jewish Torah Audio Site; Judaism 101; A Page of Talmud; Torah Study Opportunities; and Varieties of Orthodox Judaism—a *yashar koach* to each of their sponsors.

AAA Torah Discussion RECOMMENDED

http://www.milknhoney.co.il/

Thoughtfully written commentary on the weekly Torah portion and more, from an Orthodox perspective, but you don't have to be Orthodox to benefit from it. Terms and biblical concepts explained in a clear and easy-to-read manner. Recommended especially for those new to Torah study.

AishDas Society

http://aishdas.org

The AishDas Society is committed to the "advancement of meaningful worship in the Orthodox Jewish community." Its philosophy is summed up in the writings of Rabbi S. R. Hirsch, especially in his book *The Nineteen Letters*. Hirsch favored an approach he called "Torah eem derech eretz," a phrase hard to translate but one that implies respect for one's Jewishness and country. Orthodox Jews who consider themselves followers of this approach to Judaism will appreciate this site.

Hadracha

http://www.ort.org/anjy/hadracha/identity/jew-id.htm

Maintaining one's Jewish identity in a non-Jewish society is the focus of this thought-provoking website. How Jewish are we when we are indistinguishable from our Gentile neighbors in terms of dress, speech, or names? Or do these things matter? The author of this site, James Franks of the Education Department of Bnei Akiva, of Great Britain and Ireland, a religious youth group, offers questions and answers based on scripture and Jewish law.

Havienu Leshalom

http://www.havienu.org/

A "virtual congregation" based in St. Louis. The group's purposes include creating a spiritually based online community and merging "traditional chaplaincy" with the technology of the Internet. The sources it quotes are Orthodox, but I can't quite figure out who they're aiming at.

Home Page for Shuls

http://shamash.nysernet.org/shuls/shuls.html

A listing of Orthodox synagogues across the country, with hyperlinks. From Shamash, a leading provider of Jewish Internet services, based in New York.

RECOMMENDED

Hypertext Halacha

http://www.torah.org/learning/halacha/

"Halacha" means Jewish law. The most widely regarded compilation of Jewish law in recent centuries is the *Shulchan Aruch* of Rabbi Joseph Caro. The most widely regarded commentary on the *Shulchan Aruch* is by the "Chafetz Chaim," Rabbi Meir Isserles. You can find English translations of both at this site, as a hypertext document, courtesy of Project Genesis.

Ichud HaRabanim

http://www.jer1.co.il/orgs/ichud/irindex.htm

This group's full name translates roughly to "Committee of Rabbis on Behalf of the People of Israel and the Land of Israel." You'll find impassioned essays on the peace process from an Orthodox perspective.

Innernet Magazine

http://www.jer1.co.il/orgs/heritage/mag1.htm

Innernet Magazine offers articles on Judaism from a traditional point of view. It's published by Heritage House, a group of hostels in the Old City of Jerusalem. In their words, "Located in the Old City of Jerusalem, the Heritage House is privately sponsored by the international Jewish community and offers clean and modern accommodations. We welcome students and young men and women exploring Israel, and seeking to deepen their appreciation of their Jewish Heritage." You can sign up for a free subscription to their magazine at this website.

RECOMMENDED

Jewish Torah Audio Site of 613.org

http://www.613.org/

Listen to audiotape lectures (in RealAudio) about various aspects of traditional Judaism as well as recordings of traditional Jewish songs. Of special note: You can hear Rav Yoseph Soloveitchik, one of the greatest Jewish thinkers of the 20th century, speak in lectures recorded as early as the 1950s. This is by far one of the most important and exciting websites on the entire Jewish Internet. These lectures are virtually impossible to find, at any price, anywhere else. The wealth of knowledge represented here is truly astounding. This is Harvard, Yale, and Princeton all rolled into one. If you have the least interest in traditional Jewish learning, this site will get your heart racing.

RECOMMENDED

Judaism 101

http://members.aol.com/jewfaq/index.htm#Contents

Judaism 101 is an extremely cogent and well-organized guide to traditional Jewish belief. All your questions answered. Run, don't walk to this fantastic site; its author, Tracey Rich, is truly a Hero of the Jewish Internet. You'll find in-depth, thoughtfully prepared answers to difficult questions such as who is a Jew and the role of women in Judaism. You'll also meet famous scholars and sages and learn the meaning of many traditional Jewish symbols.

Kol Isha

http://www.compsoc.man.ac.uk/~jsoc/ujs/kolisha.html

> ### ♀Kol Isha - The Voice of Women
> From the Union of Jewish Students

Let's start at the beginning with this one. We have here the website of the Kol Isha campaign. Kol Isha means "Voice of the Woman" in Hebrew. Sounds normal, so far? Because after all, it's a site about Jewish feminism.

But here's the twist: In traditional Orthodox Judaism, the full phrase is "Kol Ishat Erva," meaning "the voice of a woman is lewdness." This is the justification for forbidding women to sing in public. So it's intriguing and ironic that a website written mostly, if not entirely, by and about Orthodox women from a feminist perspective would use this phrase.

These authors do not consider Orthodoxy sexist or demeaning to women. They write earnestly and frankly about how it is to be young, Orthodox, female, and thoughtful, and you'll find the page thoughtful, too. It challenges the idea that Orthodoxy and feminism have no common ground.

Legacy

http://www.legacynet.org/legnet.htm

Legacy is the Internet arm of Ohr Samayach yeshiva of Monsey, New York, an organization seeking to introduce Jews to traditional Judaism. Offering free fax subscriptions ("One page of pure inspiration delivered to you by fax every Thursday night. E-mail to Ohr@j51.com or call 1-800-OHRSOMAyach for a free subscription."), journals, seminar information, and more.

Mail-Jewish Torah and Halacha

http://www.shamash.org/mail-jewish/

An absolutely vital resource for Orthodox Jews online. Mailing lists, a phenomenal search engine, beaucoup articles, and tons more. If you're serious about halacha (Jewish law), it's tallis, tefillin, and Mail-Jewish (in that order, of course). You can discuss, via the mailing lists, Jewish topics from an Orthodox perspective. There's also a special section with material on Rav Soloveichik, one of the luminaries of 20th-century Orthodoxy, with hard-to-find lectures by the Rav and commentaries on his life and writings.

Maimonides

http://www.utexas.edu/students/cjso/Chabad/moshiach/techiya-masim.html

A lengthy and poetic analysis of Maimonides' 13 *Principles of Faith*, known in Hebrew as the *Ani Maamin*. An excerpt (yay!) from Rabbi Shmuel Boteach's book *The Wolf Shall Lie with the Lamb*. The site doesn't specify, but it appears that the book is a collection of essays by Rabbi Boteach, the Lubavitch emissary at Oxford University. If you enjoy this reference, you can click to more essays by Rabbi Boteach at a linked gopher menu.

Mordechai Torczyner's WebShas

http://www.virtual.co.il/torah/webshas/index.html

WebShas, a project of Mordechai Torczyner, is a massive and commendable project intending to provide an index to Talmudic discussions of Jewish law. In it you can find the cases, stories, and principles listed or discussed in the 363 pages (at this writing) indexed in the Babylonian Talmud. You've got to know some Talmud to benefit from it because there are many Hebrew and Aramaic terms not translated. But if you do, you can locate specific discussions with this well-organized and comprehensive index.

Orthodox Union

http://www.ou.org/

The Orthodox Union online. Information about holidays, programs, departments, and more. A massive source for Orthodox Jews. Programs include home Torah study; several different weekly D'vrai Torah (Torah commentaries); links to the National Council of Synagogue Youth (NCSY), the Orthodox Union's youth movement; a "virtual Beit Midrash," and special commentaries and programs connected to the Jewish holidays throughout the year.

A Page of Talmud

http://www.ucalgary.ca/~elsegal/TalmudPage.html#Page

This webpage is it. This is the place to learn all about the Talmud. What a breathtaking idea, and how magnificently the author, Hero of the Jewish Internet Eliezer Segal (author of "Uncle Eli's Passover Haggadah"), accomplishes his goal.

Here you'll find a picture of a page from the Talmud. Click on any part of it and you'll discover, in clear, easy-to-understand terms, everything: what it is, who wrote it, when, and why. This is the clearest, simplest, best introduction to the Talmud that I've ever seen—and what a great use of the Internet.

Awesome.

Rav Kook

http://www.ort.org/anjy/hadracha/kook/orot_en.htm

Read all about one of the leading founders of religious Zionism, Rabbi A. Y. Hakohen Kook, at this webpage. A well-written biography of one of the most influential Jews of our century and one who is hardly known outside of Orthodox circles.

Reb Shlomo Carlebach

http://www.shamash.org/judaica/rebshlomo/

They say it best: "Welcome to the deepest and most *gevaldig* place on the whole Net!" Download this website and fall under the intense scrutiny of Reb Shlomo Carlebach, the late founder of San Francisco's House of Love and Prayer, a New York synagogue, and an Israeli commune, Moshav Modi'in. Reb Shlomo brought thousands of Jews close to Judaism with his words of Torah and with his guitar. Get to know the man, his teachings, and his music (you can listen to a number of songs) here.

Reb Carlebach was the bridge between sixties activism and Jewish tradition; he also had a beautiful voice and composed countless memorable songs and melodies.

The Sepharade Page of Montreal

http://www.webcom.com/rel/welcome.html

The Sephardic community of Montreal offers essays, information, and more in both French and English. You'll find "Ask the Rav/Demander le Rav," which tackles questions of Jewish law from a traditional Talmudic and Sephardic point of view. You can also find information about trips to Morocco and a list of Sephardic synagogues in the Montreal area.

Steven Weintraub's Jewish Information Webpage

http://www.pswtech.com/~stevenw/jewish/

Learn the basics of kashrut, how to build a sukkah, and Jewish burial practices, with an excellent glossary.

Tehkelet

http://www.jer1.co.il/orgs/tekhelet/index.htm

The Association for the Promotion and Distribution of Tekhelet welcomes you to its website. What is tekhelet, you ask? And why would people form an association to promote and distribute it?

Amutat P'til Tekhelet
The Association for the Promotion and Distribution of Tekhelet
Jerusalem, Israel

There is a Biblical commandment (Numbers 15:37-39) addressed to the Children of Israel to make fringes (*tzitzit*) on the corners of their garments, for all generations. On the fringes of each corner, they are commanded to place a strand of blue (*tekhelet*). Upon seeing this strand of *tekhelet*, they will remember all the commandments of G-d, and they will do them.

What is Tekhelet?

Orthodox Jewish men wear a four-cornered garment known as a "tallit katan" or "little prayer shawl" under their shirts. Like the big prayer shawl used in religious services, the little shawl has attached, at each corner, an extremely complex series of strings and knots, symbolic of the commandments from the Bible.

One of the commandments of the Bible is that one of the strings on each corner of the prayer shawl, large or small, should be of a particular blue-purple color. That color is known in the Bible as "tekhelet."

And that's the problem. Over the millennia, the precise color and nature of tekhelet has been lost. So Jews today use only white strings. Enter, however, the Association for the Promotion and Distribution of Tekhelet. They are doing research into just what that bluish-purple color was. That way, Jews will be able to have a blue thread along with the white, as the Bible commands.

Any questions? Don't ask me. I've just exhausted my knowledge on the subject. Why not visit this website and ask the experts.

Temple Institute

http://www.actcom.co.il/jerusalem/

A somewhat bizarre yet extremely dedicated organization, the Temple Institute seeks to raise "Temple consciousness" among Jews. The Temple Institute wants to make Jews aware of the importance of building the Third Temple, ushering in the era of the Messiah, on the site of the first two Temples in Jerusalem. Of course, two large Moslem mosques stand on that spot right now, so this is definitely a challenging project from an architectural point of view.

Torah and Derekh Eretz

http://www.users.interport.net/~lisa/judaism.html

A lively and opinionated, not to say combative and rambunctious, presentation of the basics of Orthodox belief. By Lisa Aaronson.

Torah Commentaries

http://www.cyberscribe.com/tt/index.shtml

Weekly commentaries on the Torah portion, aliyah by aliyah, from the Israel Center, the Jerusalem home of the Orthodox Union.

Torah Commentary

http://www.jer1.co.il/lists/parasha-page/

Literate, scholarly, and enjoyable weekly commentaries on the Torah portion. Subscribe for free to the wisdom of Mordecai Kornfeld, a religious Jew who makes his home in Har Nof, Jerusalem.

Kornfeld writes his commentaries for newcomers and scholars alike, and presents a variety of approaches—everything from Talmudic and Midrashic commentaries to Gematria and grammatical analysis. If that last sentence means nothing to you, read Kornfeld's work, and in a very short time, you'll be an expert, too.

Torah from Dixie Plantation

http://home.navisoft.com/tfd/frontpage.htm

Shalom, y'all, from the Torah from Dixie Plantation. Apparently some observant Atlantans wanted to clear up some misconceptions about Judaism south of the Mason-Dixon line. To combat those ignorant Northern perceptions, they now offer commentary on the Torah and more. Stop on by for some southern Jewish hospitality.

One of my college roommates came from Savannah, Georgia. His grandmother was meticulous in her observance of the laws of kashrut, he told us, with one small exception: shrimp. "God," she'd say, in her Southern accent, "could never have meant for those cute little things not to be kosher!"

Torah Study Opportunities

http://shamash.org/reform/uahc/congs/dc/dc001/torahnet.html

One of the most important websites, period. Hero of the Jewish Internet Eric Simon has compiled an astonishingly large list of Torah study opportunities via Web, e-mail subscription, and gopher. You can listen to audio classes, subscribe to daily or weekly e-mail lectures on a wide variety of Torah topics, and discover other Torah study opportunities. Simon has provided a wonderful service by pulling together all these diverse sources and organizing them so well.

Traditional Prayer

gopher://gopher.torah.org/hh/lists/tefila

This gopher menu offers lengthy, anonymous essays on various aspects of traditional prayer. You'll find line-by-line analysis of morning prayers, religious aspects of Jewish holidays, and essays on the meaning and purpose of prayer. This site will make more sense to a reader with some previous Torah background. One certainly wonders who the anonymous author is.

Varieties of Orthodox Judaism   RECOMMENDED

http://www.ucalgary.ca/~elsegal/363_Transp/08_Orthodoxy.html#Map

Hero of the Internet Eliezer Segal strikes again, this time with a description of each of the movements and leaders within Orthodox Judaism. Well researched and attractively presented, this website will show you that Orthodoxy is hardly a monolithic entity. A well-designed chart shows you the history of Orthodox movements—where they began, whether in Poland, Lithuania, Germany, or elsewhere; who or what yeshiva was influential, and how it evolved. Click on any group and read a brief, informative essay on that group. Fascinating.

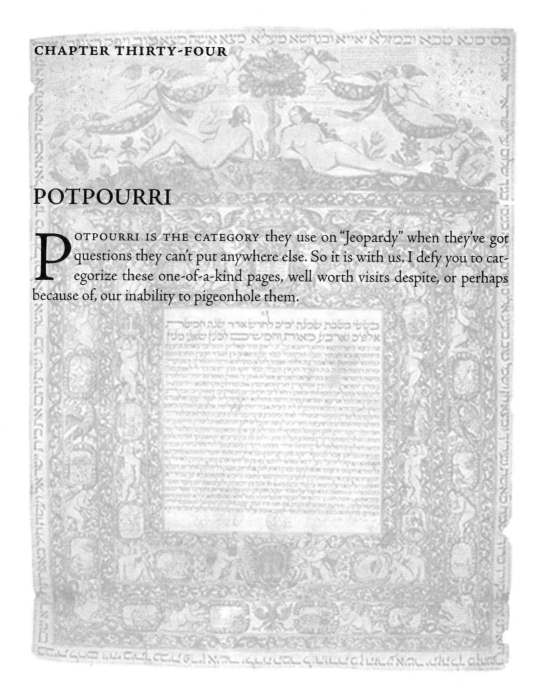

CHAPTER THIRTY-FOUR

POTPOURRI

POTPOURRI IS THE CATEGORY they use on "Jeopardy" when they've got questions they can't put anywhere else. So it is with us. I defy you to categorize these one-of-a-kind pages, well worth visits despite, or perhaps because of, our inability to pigeonhole them.

Calendar

http://shamash.nysernet.org/cal.html

A Hebrew calendar for the month, and other data, like sunrise and sunset in New York and today's Hebrew date. Simple but highly useful for Jews who need to know times for Sabbath observance and daily prayers.

Calendar of Jewish Holidays

http://bnaibrith.org/caln.html

Seven years of Jewish holidays in an easy-to-read chart. Now you can plan Passover in the year 2002. From the B'nai B'rith.

Chicken Soup

http://www.users.interport.net/~cuposoup/chicken.html

If you have a virtual head cold, tune in here and view a picture of a virtual bowl of chicken soup. Hey, I told you this stuff was miscellaneous.

English and Hebrew Calendar

http://www.math.grin.edu/~nogradi/calendar/

An attractive and useful English and Hebrew calendar, courtesy of Chabad Lubavitch of Iowa.

Famous Jews

http://ucsu.colorado.edu/~jsu/cgi-bin/famous.cgi

Win bets and amaze your friends as you play "Who is a Jew?" You'll find the names of famous Jews in all fields, including sports, business, entertainment, fashion, politics, and upholstering. From the Ultimate Jewish/Israel Link Launcher, by Hero of the Jewish Internet Steve Ruttenberg.

Free Fax Service

http://www.gold.net.il/~may/fax.htm

The Israel Internet Key, an Israeli service provider, lets you send faxes for free via the Internet, even if you're not in Israel, with Tel Aviv–based Inter-Fax. Find out how here.

Israel's Basic Laws

http://www.uni-hamburg.de/law/is__indx.html

Israel does not have a written constitution. Instead, it has these laws, collectively referred to as its Basic Laws. They cover pretty much the same sorts of things as does the U.S. Constitution. You can order a set of the laws here.

Jewish Book News and Reviews

http://www.ort.org/communit/jbook/start.htm

Here's a site for Jewish book lovers. This home page of British journal *Jewish Book News and Reviews* is published three times a year. It offers background information and lists of Jewish books reviewed in recent issues.

The Lower East Side   RECOMMENDED

http://140.190.128.190/SMC/Dept/history/Contents.html

The old Lower East Side of New York City, turn-of-the-century home to hundreds of thousands of Jews, comes to life in this fascinating, well-chosen collection of articles and essays.

Nice Jewish Boy Page

http://www.amherst.edu/~bslinker/njb/menu.html

The Cult of the Nice Jewish Boy. A page paying homage to Famous Nice Jewish Boys, Nice Jewish Boys I Know, Nice Jewish Boys in America, and Nice Jewish Boys Worldwide.

With a link to the Nice Jewish Girls website. No kidding.

Sefer—Israeli Book Club

http://www.netvision.net.il/~ancient/

Sefer, the Israeli book club, will locate any Hebrew book for you. Sign up and get the monthly list of books from all publishers on all topics. You can also buy books as a member of the club; joining is free.

Thinking Jewish, Acting Jewish

http://bc.emanon.net/daffodils/

Thinking Jewish, Acting Jewish is a monthly magazine for Jews interested in "self-directed Jewish life." At the site, you'll find excerpts and articles about Israel and aspects of Judaism culled from Israeli and American publications, as well as original pieces. Topics include the Ninth of Av, a day of tragedy and mourning in the Jewish calendar; the writings of Zionist author Ahad HaAm, and how to find good bagels in Tel Aviv.

Top-12 Lists

http://www.jcn18.com/t-120001.htm#COMMAND

This service of the Jewish Communications Network offers TOP-12 lists of all things Jewish. David Letterman-like humor; some of it's funny and some of it is just okay. For example, one recent item from a top-12 list was "Israel's national hockey team participated in the 1992 Olympics, dominating both the Olympic Village and the concession area." Get it?

Hey, they're trying. Add your own top-12 list, if you like.

CHAPTER THIRTY-FIVE

PROGRESSIVE AND RECONSTRUCTIONIST JUDAISM

ENCOMPASSING THE HAVURAH MOVEMENT and Humanistic Judaism. Nontraditional and nontheistic Judaism takes many forms; you can get a sense of the options from these sites. You'll find congregations, articles, magazines, gopher menus, prayer services, and online learning opportunities. Each of these branches of Judaism is relatively new and therefore in some degree of flux; the Internet offers those who identify with these new approaches to Judaism a chance to communicate and work out the philosophy and details. Interestingly, Reform Judaism started much the same way in the early 19th century in Germany—congregations sprung up, came into contact, and eventually worked out a common approach. The Internet will surely hasten that process for these more recent developments in Jewish religious and community life.

Egalitarian Wedding Contract

http://www.cs.engr.uky.edu/~raphael/yiddish/ksubo.gif

An "egalitarian kesubo" or wedding contract—alas, not translated from the Hebrew—by Raphael Fink and Michael Fox. The traditional kesubah provides that a woman is entitled to financial support in the marriage and in the event of divorce; this version presumably gives both parties equal rights and responsibilities. No special downloading skills necessary; just type in the URL and it will appear in its entirety.

Heart of Texas Havurah

http://www.cs.utexas.edu/users/ubiquity/jewish/jhot.html

Meet the Heart of Texas Havurah at its Austin home and learn about their scheduled services, events, and parties. The Havurah movement brings together about a dozen couples or families in a neighborhood or city and allows them to create their own means of expressing their Jewishness.

Human Development Institute

http://shamash.org/judaica/hdi/index.html

The Human Development Institute blends mystical and practical Judaism with New Age thinking. You'll find weekly spiritual insights and long-distance learning opportunities as well as audiovisual tools. The founder, Rabbi Laibl Wolf, describes himself as an Orthodox Chasidic Jew and a "Jewish exponent of the universal pathway."

Humanistic Judaism

http://www.teleport.com/~hellman/

Humanistic Judaism is the movement for Jews who wish to identify with Judaism "in a nontheistic manner." Learn about this form of Judaism, join their mailing lists, and meet members here.

RECOMMENDED

Humanistic Judaism: Background

http://www.jmas.co.jp/FAQs/judaism/reading-lists/humanistic

Look here in this FAQ excerpt for some background and recommended reading on the Humanistic Judaism movement. Provided by Daniel Faigin, Hero of the Jewish Internet. The introductory essay is extremely well written and worthy of your time. Definitely a consciousness-expanding experience.

RECOMMENDED

Humanistic Judaism: Congregation Beth Adam

http://www.bethadam.org/index.html#aboutbeth

Congregation Beth Adam of Cincinnati, Ohio, offers well-reasoned and articulate explanations of Humanistic Judaism's philosophy and theology. This congregation takes clear stands on the very challenging issues of what Humanistic Judaism is and what a Humanistic Jewish congregation does. This is a well-written and attractive page and serves as a fine starting point for anyone who wants to learn about Humanistic Judaism.

Humanistic Judaism Gopher Menu

gopher://israel.nysernet.org:70/1m/renewal/aleph/archives

The dedicated cybergoer can root around in these searchable gopher files and find interesting information about Humanistic Judaism, Arthur Waskow, and the Jewish Revival movement. I use the term "dedicated" because when you click in, you get five choices, all of which read "Fwd: ALEPH material for W.W.W." **Hint:** Try the third one. You'll get information about ALEPH, the Alliance for Jewish Renewal, based in Philadelphia. A little bit of indexing would make this site considerably more useful and accessible.

Humanistic Judaism Mailing List

http://www.teleport.com/~hellman/subscrip.html

You can subscribe to the Humanistic Judaism mailing list by sending e-mail to majordomo@teleport.com. Leave the message's "subject" blank (or put in your first and last name). Type the following into the body of the message:

    subscribe hj
    end

You can find out more details at their website listed here.

The Jewish Reconstructionist Federation

http://shamash.NYSerNet.ORG/jrf/

Essays on Reconstructionist Judaism and articles from *The Recon-structionist*, the movement's publication. You'll find discussions on topics like: "Perhaps You Are a Reconstructionist?" "What Is Reconstructionism?" and "Religious Pluralism in Israel." Also here: links to Reconstructionist congregations with websites, and an explanation of how to affiliate with Reconstructionist Judaism.

K'hillat Keddem

http://www.next.com/~amarcum/keddem.html

K'hillat Keddem of Palo Alto, California welcomes you to its home page. Founding principles, announcements, and newsletters make this attractive home page a model for other congregations thinking about going online.

Leyv Ha-Ir (Heart of the City)

http://www.netaxs.com/~stessa/ccrs.html

Leyv Ha-Ir, Hebrew for "Heart of the City," is center city Philadelphia's Reconstructionist congregation. Meet them here and discover some local traditions you might want to borrow for your Jewish community.

Mordecai Kaplan, Founder of the Reconstruction Movement

http://www.chattanooga.net/~tpkunesh/atheism.f/kaplan.htm

Here's a brief biography of Mordecai Kaplan, founder of the Reconstructionist movement and author of *Judaism as a Civilization*.

Or Hadash Congregation

http://www.libertynet.org/~orhadash/index.html

Learn some of the basics of the Reconstructionist movement at the home page of Or Hadash Congregation in Fort Washington, Pennsylvania.

Reconstructionist Rabbinical College

http://www.expresso.com/rrc/catalog2.htm

The Reconstructionist Rabbinical College, located outside Philadelphia, Pennsylvania, offers a five-year program leading to rabbinical ordination. Learn about the movement, the school, and the program.

Shabbat Evening Service

http://math.bu.edu/INDIVIDUAL/samuel/service-women.html

Here's the text of a shabbat evening service, compiled by Geri Garfinkel, for the Progressive Havurah, Boston, Massachusetts. Poetry, prayer, and traditional liturgy. You can use the entire service or borrow aspects to create your own. The Progressive Havurah is a religious community with a nontraditional approach to Jewish tradition, or so one might conclude from a reading of this service.

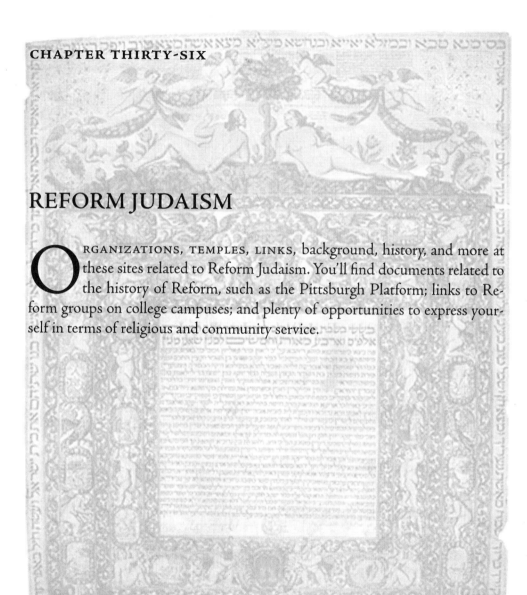

CHAPTER THIRTY-SIX

REFORM JUDAISM

ORGANIZATIONS, TEMPLES, LINKS, background, history, and more at these sites related to Reform Judaism. You'll find documents related to the history of Reform, such as the Pittsburgh Platform; links to Reform groups on college campuses; and plenty of opportunities to express yourself in terms of religious and community service.

Hebrew Union College

http://www.shamash.org/reform/uahc/congs/ot/ot002/

Founded in 1875, Hebrew Union College (HUC) is the leading Reform Jewish seminary, and now it's online. HUC is the central training institute for leaders in the Reform Jewish community. Web voyagers can learn about their new "Rhythms of Jewish Life," a weekly e-mail discussion group, and search their telephone, fax, and e-mail directory.

Hillel   RECOMMENDED

http://shamash.nysernet.org/hillel/

The Foundation for Jewish Campus Life

Hillel is the collegiate home of Judaism, and their home page is vast and informative. You'll find information about the organization itself, a listing of Hillels on campuses worldwide, and online discussion groups.

Kesher

http://www.netspace.org/~mharvey/kesher/#WhatIs

College students can connect with Kesher, a nationwide organiza-tion for Reform Judaism on campus, at this site. With contact names, e-mail links, and more.

RECOMMENDED

Reform Judaism

http://shamash.nysernet.org/reform/

A home page for the Reform movement, offering links to a variety of leading Reform organizations such as the American Confer-ence of Cantors, the Women of Reform Judaism, and the North American Federation of Temple Youth (NFTY). But perhaps most impressive is their tour of Reform Judaism on the Web, an anno-tated guide to the most important Reform Jewish Internet resources. Education, congregations, highlights of the best websites, archives, and convention information—you can find all of it here, quickly and easily.

RECOMMENDED

Reform Judaism Home Page

http://www.con.wesleyan.edu/~slinky/refjud.html

A resource that overlaps only slightly with the previous entry in this section. Here you will find more than a dozen clickable ini-tials such as UAHC (Union of American Hebrew Congregations); HUC–JIR (Hebrew Union College–Jewish Institute of Religion); and CCAR (Central Conference of American Rabbis). In short, one-stop shopping for all the leading organizations and institutions of Reform Judaism.

Reform Judaism Reading List

http://shamash.nysernet.org/lists/scj-faq/HTML/rl/jlu-index.html

This portion of the soc.culture.jewish FAQ (see Chapter 14), the most important resource on the entire Jewish Internet and the brainchild of Hero of the Jewish Internet Daniel P. Faigin, offers essays on the following topics related to Reform Judaism: beliefs; rituals and practice; liturgy; responsa; and history; as well as discussions of the Bible and the Reform Rabbinate. Exciting, well-written, not to be missed.

Religious Action Committee

http://shamash.nysernet.org/reform/rac/index.html

The Religious Action Committee (RAC) pursues social justice and religious liberty in the United States. The RAC follows legislation and seeks to mobilize the American Jewish community. Read about their programs and their latest news and announcements here. Welfare reform, foreign aid, political advocacy by religious groups—if it happens in the world of politics, you can read about it here.

Service/Song Archive

http://www.netspace.org/~dmacks/shira/

The Service/Song Archive, by Daniel Macks, lets you put together a Reform Jewish service with no fuss, no muss. An excellent archive of Hebrew and English texts for just about any aspect of the service you can think of. A great resource and easy to use: Download their shareware one time and then click on a portion of the service. You'll get text that you can edit into a service you're putting together. Then you and your congregation can essentially customize a service to your own liking. The Reform service offers a lot of room for experimenting; you'll find tons of new options here.

RECOMMENDED

UAHC Internet Resources

http://shamash.nysernet.org/reform/uahc/resources.html

The Union of American Hebrew Congregations maintains this useful list of Internet resources for Reform Judaism. Newsgroups and mailing lists available here include temple-chat, discussions among leaders of UAHC congregations; ccrjdgrp, discussions within the Canadian Council for Reform Judaism; mail.liberal-judaism, topics about liberal Judaism moderated by Daniel Faigin; and "NATE," a resource offering discussions about Reform Jewish education.

Union of American Hebrew Congregations

http://shamash.org/reform/uahc/index.html

Everything you always wanted to know about the Union of American Hebrew Congregations, the synagogue arm of Reform Judaism. Includes the name, location, phone number, and link to the home page of every UAHC congregation in the United States.

You can also find policy statements about Reform Judaism, a complete listing of officers and departments, news about new publications, and the text of such key Reform Judaism documents as the Pittsburgh Platform of 1885.

CHAPTER THIRTY-SEVEN

SINGLES

WHAT'S WRONG, BUNKY? Late nights spent alone downloading naughty pictures from the Internet? Not anymore! Find a partner or simply a pen pal at these websites dedicated to helping Jewish people meet one another. We can't vouch for the credibility of the commercial sites, and frankly, some of them look a little doubtful. But many legitimate organizations here, organized alphabetically, offer all kinds of events for the unattached. If you meet your mate through *The Guide to the Jewish Internet*, be sure to FedEx us a slice of wedding cake.

After visiting all of the sites described below, I have a little more respect for the free ones than for the pay services. In Judaism, to introduce two people who get married is to be *m'shutaf im ha-Kaddosh baruch-hu*, a partner with God. I respect the people who do this work for love and not for money, but everybody's got to make a living. And you might even see a commercial service that strikes you as worth the investment, so we list both kinds. Happy hunting!

Atlanta Jewish Community Center, Atlanta, Georgia

http://www.acme-atlanta.com/clubs/ajcc/

Candor by Candlelight is just one of the many activities for singles offered by the Atlanta Jewish Community Center. Volleyball, the Newcomers Network, and An Evening in Monte Carlo offer single Jews in Atlanta the chance to meet. Visit the page and experience the graciousness.

Chai Center, Los Angeles, California   RECOMMENDED

http://www.otn.com/chaicenter/

Rabbi Shlomo and Olivia Schwartz, who run the nonprofit Chai Center, are extremely nice people committed to teaching about Judaism and helping single Jews meet in a pleasant, intelligent atmosphere. They provide all sorts of events for single Jewish Angelenos and are known for their shabbat Dinner for 30 Strangers. They offer couples clubs, singles parties, shabbat dinners, holiday celebrations, communal Passover seders, classes, lectures, counseling, and rabbinical officiation at life-cycle events. Their activities are for "Conservative, Reform, non-affiliates, and any Jew that moves!"

Detroit Jewish Community, Detroit, Michigan

http://www.metroguide.com/jewishweb/person.html

Everything you need to know about the Detroit Jewish community, with a singles page that spans the 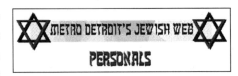 Jewish world. Read and respond to the many listings here, or post your own for free.

Greater Seattle Jewish Community

http://jewishinseattle.org/calendar/calendar.htm#Apr1996

Seattle's kind of a subtle place, so the "Jewish in Seattle" home page doesn't list a singles section per se. But you'll probably find something to suit your tastes on their events calendar. Visit the JCC Singles Hotline Online for Seattle for specifically singles events.

Events sponsored include Earthquake Night at the Kingdome. Just kidding.

A Group of Jewish Singles, New Jersey Area

http://www.monmouth.com/~hpkatseff/agojs/

More than 40 congregations and Jewish organizations combine to bring you A Group of Jewish Singles, which offers a wide variety of activities for Jewish folk of all ages. There's a special emphasis on outdoorsy stuff with JOGS, the Jewish Outdoor Group of Singles.

Haskalah@west london, England

http://www.ort.org/anjy/orgtions/haskalah/haskalah.htm

Jewish singles in London and visitors to the U.K. can meet and greet via Haskalah@west london, a group for Jews 25–35 meeting Thursday evenings at West London Synagogue in Central London. Haskalah plans to link up with other Jewish groups in the same age range for social events including weekends away both in the U.K. and in other countries. Haskalah claims to be the only independent group for Jewish singles 25–35 in the U.K. Find out more about them and their activities here.

How to Use Internet Personals

http://www.lib.ox.ac.uk:80/internet/news/faq/alt.personals.jewish.html

Advice on how to use Internet personal ads in this FAQ entitled "One straight male's thoughts and advice on successful Usenet personals." The author writes that he had "ended a devastating relationship with a very nasty person" and turned to the Internet for solace. He promptly met "a beautiful woman who was my lover for about six weeks. We're still friends." Isn't that special. He then met the woman who became his wife. How he did it—and how you can, too.

Israel Chat

http://lynx.dac.neu.edu:8000/~dweinber/israel.couples.html

The Official Israel Couples Page is a webpage dedicated to the question of whether Israelis can find love over the Internet. Still in the infatuation stage, this site promises IRC (chat room) and other Internet love connections. Just what American parents need: lonely Israeli men trying to make contact with their daughters.

Jewish Activity Center of the South Bay, Los Angeles, California

http://members.aol.com/sbayjewact/

You get a friendly feeling from the people who bring you the webpage of the Jewish Activity Center of the South Bay, which comprises the beach communities between Palos Verdes and El Segundo. Their schedule includes coffee cartels, hikes, bike trips, and other events. Check it out. Easy-to-read maps if you're new to the area.

Jewish Adult and Graduate Student Society, Cambridge, Massachusetts

http://hcs.harvard.edu:80/~hrhillel/jagss/jagss.html

Grad students at Harvard and MIT as well as young Jewish adults in the area are welcome at events sponsored by the Jewish Adult and Graduate Student Society. These events include shabbat dinners, movies, hikes, ski trips, and other such. You don't have to be an intellectual, either. You just have to not mind listening to them talk.

Jewish Bulletin of Northern California

http://www.jewish.com:80/bk960308/pers.htm

Is ANYBODY married in the San Francisco Bay area? You'd never think it when you see how many Jewish singles advertise on this website sponsored by the *Jewish Bulletin* of Northern California. And visit their listing of singles groups, matchmaking services, and "not just for singles" groups throughout the Bay Area at http://www.jewish.com:80/bk960308/pagehome.htm. Also, visit their website at http://www.jewish.com/resource/ch10.htm where you'll find a chapter from their free publication titled *Resource: A Guide to Jewish Life in Northern California*. Well worth a cybervisit.

Jewish Connections

http://www.jewishconnections.com/

This singles service, Jewish Connections, offers matchmaking to Jews in the Delaware Valley, which they broadly define as Washington, D.C., Delaware, New Jersey, Pennsylvania, and New York. Find out about them or fill out a query form at their site.

Jewish Quality Singles

http://www.thenet.net/~singles/service.htm

Pay them $75 and you can meet and mingle with the "Jewish Quality Singles" at this website. With the moderately ambitious goal of listing Jewish singles events for every city in the world, in case you're lonely *and* you have a whole mess of frequent flier miles.

Jewish Singles Connection   RECOMMENDED

http://www.zdepth.com/jsc/index.html

A lot of work went into this site, and the results are impressive. You'll find lists of Jewish singles groups and publications; colleges, Hillels, student groups, and fraternities and sororities; travel opportunities for Jewish singles; and individual postings. This is a very thorough compilation of Jewish singles resources throughout the U.S., Canada, and the U.K., with links to a wide variety of Jewish singles websites. You'll also find personal ads from individuals, and you can post your own for free. An excellent resource.

Jewish Singles Searching, Rochester and Western and Central New York

http://www.roccplex.com/jss

Jewish Singles Searching is an independent, nonprofit social group for Jewish singles 25–50 years old. Join them for theater evenings, picnics, dances, holiday parties, and other events. Find out more about them here.

Jewish Visual Profile

http://www.bridge.net/jewish-p/personal/

For a fee, this commercial site, the Jewish Visual Profile, promises to let you gaze upon the countenances of "eligible Jewish men and women who are serious about being in a committed relationship within the next 12 months."

JNFY, Melbourne, Australia

http://www.wej.com.au/jnfy/

They know how to party down under. JNFY is the branch of the Jewish National Fund (JNF) for people in their 20s and 30s, operating in Sydney and Melbourne, Australia. Throughout the year they hold social and educational functions that cater to this age group. Like the time that more than 400 Jewish

Aussies gathered in an art gallery to launch the JNFY, with a jazz quartet playing merrily in the background. Visit JFNY's page to find out more about them and their activities.

Matzo Ball

http://www.jewishsingles.com/matzobal/

The Matzo Ball, sponsored by *Visual Profile* magazine (see Jewish Visual Profile), offers large parties in big cities across the U.S., and singles cruises, too. It's actually a pretty smart idea—these entrepreneurs rent out large dance clubs in cities with big Jewish populations, but they do it on Christmas Eve and other nights when Jews are likely to have few entertainment options. The parties attract thousands; you can join their group and receive discounts. Learn how here.

Midwest Jewish Connection

http://members.gnn.com/hca/mjc/index.htm

Although it's mostly Minnesota, you'll find free personal ads, a singles directory, and a directory of Jewish social foundations and services here.

Osher, Los Angeles Area

http://uscj.org/pacsw/osher.html

The United Synagogue of Conservative Judaism tell us that *osher*, Hebrew for "happiness," is derived from love (*ahavah*), peace (*shalom*), and friendship (*ray-ut*). Singles 21–37 can check out their listings of social events and find some *osher* for themselves.

Stroum Jewish Community Center, Seattle, Washington

http://www.jewishinseattle.org/jcc/singles.htm

Book clubs, movie clubs, theater nights, klezmer. Whatever you want, if you're sleeping single in Seattle, you'll have no excuse any more. Check out your many options here.

Travel to Israel

http://www.usyd.edu.au/~hconyer/Rendezvous.html

Singles over 30 can travel to Israel in search of sun, history, and romance, not necessarily in that order.

United Synagogue Computer Service, Los Angeles, California

http://www.uscj.org/pacsw/sngls.html

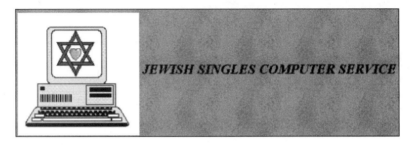

Since 1977 the nonprofit United Synagogue Computer Service has been helping Jewish singles find the mates of their choice. They serve the Los Angeles and Orange County areas and claim that more than 12,000 singles have used their system, resulting in hundreds of marriages. For a $60 fee they promise three computer printouts, each listing up to five names with phone numbers. Find out more about them or send them e-mail from their website.

Young Professionals Kesher, Washington, D.C.

http://www.access.digex.net/~erics/ypk.html#top

This attractive and energetic website presents the Young Professionals Kesher, a group for singles and marrieds in their 20s and 30s who want to meet other Jews their age and build a sense of Jewish community.

The group addresses itself specifically to those young Jews who feel shut out of traditional synagogue life, and it holds social and politically minded events throughout Washington and the Northern Virginia area.

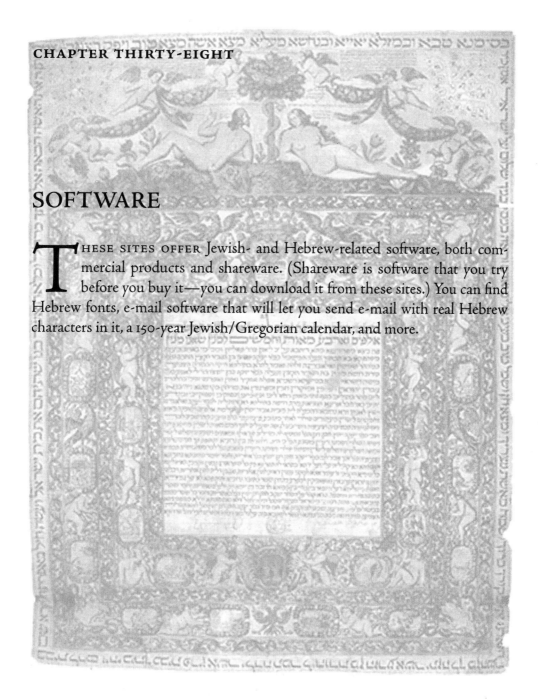

CHAPTER THIRTY-EIGHT

SOFTWARE

THESE SITES OFFER Jewish- and Hebrew-related software, both commercial products and shareware. (Shareware is software that you try before you buy it—you can download it from these sites.) You can find Hebrew fonts, e-mail software that will let you send e-mail with real Hebrew characters in it, a 150-year Jewish/Gregorian calendar, and more.

150-Year Calendar

http://www.virtual.co.il/city_services/calendar/oz/

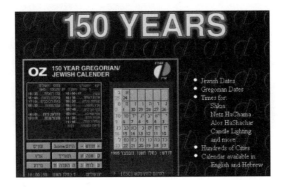

Download a limited working version of this 150-year Gregorian/Jewish calendar, complete with times for Jewish prayer. Or buy the whole thing.

All About Reading Hebrew on the Web   RECOMMENDED

http://www.reshet.com/hebrew.htm

Visit this site for everything you need to know about reading Hebrew on the Web. You can download and install free Hebrew fonts, and you can also find an excellent FAQ with answers to these questions: (1) Is there a standard? (2) Why do Hebrew characters show "backward" on my screen? (3) Why does the Web Hebrew standard differ from plain Hebrew standard? (4) What are some sites that use Hebrew? (5) What about the ACCENT Hebrew plug-in? and (6) What do I do if my spouse runs off with a computer-literate Israeli?

All kidding aside, our panel of experts voted this site the most user-friendly of all those in this section. I wonder how you say "download" in Hebrew.

RECOMMENDED

All the Jewish Software You'll Ever Need

http://www.davka.com/

It's not free, but it's not just Hebrew fonts either. Visit Davka Corporation's site and you'll read about Jewish-oriented software you may never have dreamed of. This is the largest developer and distributor of Hebrew and Judaic software for personal computers. PC and Mac users welcome. You'll find everything imaginable in Hebrew/English word processing tools, CD-ROMs, fonts, graphics, Hebrew language stuff, and "fun & games." You can also request a catalog or become a Beta Tester.

RECOMMENDED

E-mail in Hebrew

http://www.hevanet.com/dshivers/mikhtav

Download free software here enabling you to send e-mail with Hebrew characters (for Macintosh, DOS, and Windows). Pretty cool. Also, an intriguing essay on the question of reading from right to left on the Internet.

Hebrew Fonts

http://www1.snunit.k12.il/snunit/heb.html/

Teach your computer to read Hebrew. Find out where to download Hebrew fonts and how to install them, for Macintosh, Windows, and UNIX.

Hebrew Fonts for Macs

http://www.mid.net/INFO-MAC/

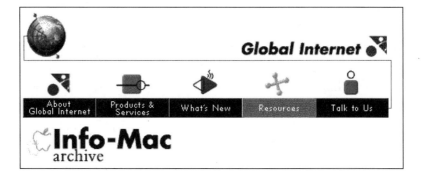

Search this archive for information and software that will let you read Hebrew on your Macintosh.

Jewish Shareware

http://jewishpost.nais.com/jewishpost/judaic2.html#galore

This site, sponsored by the *Jewish Post* of New York, offers Jewish shareware (Macintosh and Windows) such as a perpetual Jewish calendar, Hebrew text fonts, even a Jewish screen saver.

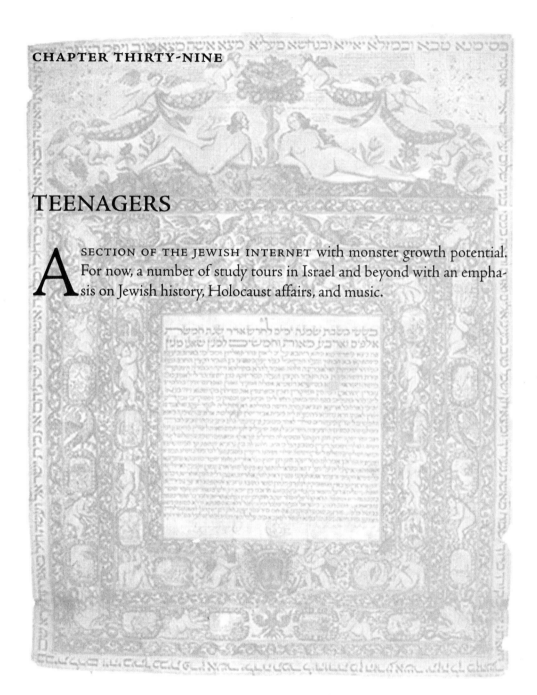

CHAPTER THIRTY-NINE

TEENAGERS

A SECTION OF THE JEWISH INTERNET with monster growth potential. For now, a number of study tours in Israel and beyond with an emphasis on Jewish history, Holocaust affairs, and music.

Alexander Muss High School

http://www.amhsi.com/

An attractive home page setting forth the benefits of this American high school in Israel. This page appeals both to reason and to emotion, which is to say that both parents and teenagers will like it. The school, located in Hod Ha'Sharon, is an alternative for American students of high school age, and entices visitors to its webpage with things to click on like "You'll find this nowhere else!" "You figure it out!" "Top 10 reasons," and "Now what?" A model webpage for schools seeking students and students seeking schools.

Bronfman Youth Fellowships in Israel

http://shamash.nysernet.org/byfi/index.html

The Bronfman Youth Fellowships in Israel are made possible by financial support from the Samuel Bronfman Foundation, Inc. Their program is designed to send to Israel each summer an outstanding group of incoming high school seniors from a variety of Jewish backgrounds who return home wanting to know more about their people, traditions, religion, and culture. Learn more about the fellowships here.

Hazimir

http://www.azc.com/client/sheri/hazamir/

Hazimir, the National Jewish High School Choir, travels to Israel to tour and sing. The group has outposts throughout the mid-Atlantic states and Boston. Visit their site for more information on the group and to send them a message.

RECOMMENDED

Jerusalem Through the Windows of Time

http://www.jer1.co.il/orgs/ped/jerintro.html

Jerusalem Through the Windows of Time, a beautifully written book for older children by Abraham Stahl, is excerpted in great length at this website of the Joint Authority for Jewish Zionist Education. Moving discussions, poetry, and teaching activities focused on the Jew's traditional love of Jerusalem. This is an example of how the Internet benefits everyone—kids, teachers, authors, organizations. If you teach or sell to teenagers, you can get some great ideas on how to post things by looking at this site.

Jewish Youth Information League   RECOMMENDED

http://www.intac.com/~manning/jewishyouth/

The Jewish Youth Information League provides information, statements, and maps about the dangers its authors recognize for Jewish young people. These include religious groups that attempt to convert Jews to Christianity, Aryan extremist movements, Islamic fundamentalist groups, and the Nation of Islam. Pointed and frightening. Articles include a message from Elie Wiesel and topics such as "The Silent Religious Holocaust of Russian Jews," "Learn About the Evangelical Insult at Auschwitz," "The Ideological Lies Disseminated by Hebrew Christians," and "Why Jews Can't Believe in Jesus."

Swedish March of the Living

http://www.algonet.se/~hatikva/motl.english.html

The Swedish March of the Living is a two-week trip to Poland and Israel for 6,000 Jewish young people, to commemorate the Holocaust and the birth of the State of Israel, "the two most important events of Jewish history [in] this century." At the website you'll get the basics about how to participate in this event. The event is sponsored by the Swedish Jewish community.

Teen Israel Experience

http://www.shamash.org/teenisrl/

Y ou're a teen. You want to get away from your parents, and who can blame you. Why not spend a large chunk of their hard-earned money on *yourself*? The Israel Experience offers a wide variety of study and other sorts of tours to Israel, with specialties from scuba diving to archaeology. An excellent search engine allows you to find the trip that's best for you. You can limit the search by participant's age; length of time away; school age; and special features such as Bar/Bat Mitzvah, outdoor adventure, or service opportunities (for college-age students). For example, I clicked on Bar/Bat Mitzvah programs for junior high school–age students and found six matches. A typical match: a two week program run by the Department of Jewish Education and Culture in the Diaspora. I clicked on that group and got an address, phone number, e-mail address, and links to other programs.

Travel to Israel

http://shamash.nysernet.org/reform/uahc/israel.html

T ravel to Israel for teens and college students sponsored by the Reform Jewish National Federation of Temple Youth (NFTY). Programs specialize in archaeology, nature sites, the arts, learning Hebrew, community service, and other themes; longer-term, semester, and year trips are also available. A telephone contact is provided for further information. This is a fairly brief (one page) site, but it gets you started. No links to other groups' tours.

CHAPTER FORTY

TRAVEL

ARE YOU LOOKING FOR A CHANGE this Passover? Would you like to spend Passover in Cannes, perhaps? How about traveling to China in search of Chinese Jewish history? Whatever you desire, these websites introduce you to Jewish-oriented travel around the world. From medically oriented trips to take with fellow physicians, to a trip to Poland to study pre-Holocaust Eastern European Jewish communities, you can find out how here.

Beit Hashita

http://www.ultranet.com/~rleavitt/beithashita/

American 10th and 11th graders can spend a year on a kibbutz with this program. Kibbutz Beit Hashita is located at the base of Mount Gilboa in "the fertile Jezreel Valley." Students will be "adopted" into kibbutz families and absorbed into Israeli culture and life. Information about the program, and a little bit about the kibbutz, at this site. This kibbutz has always been one of Israel's largest agricultural settlements, with 10,000 acres under cultivation. If you want to help Israel grow anything from chickpeas to watermelon, this is your kibbutz.

China Judaic Studies Association   RECOMMENDED

http://www.oakton.edu/~friend/chinajews.html

Judaic Studies in China is the topic of this Illinois-based webpage. Learn about university courses, tours to China, awards, and related publications, such as *The Jews of Shanghai* by author Pan Guang. An essay entitled "A Visit to Kaifeng" by Beverly Friend offers an interesting introduction to Chinese Jewish history and is well worth reading.

Globe Corner Bookstore

http://www.gcb.com/catalog/g/i530.html

The Globe Corner Bookstore in Boston and Cambridge, Massachusetts, offers you previews and ordering information for a variety of titles on touring in Israel and beyond.

Hazamir

http://www.azc.com/client/sheri/hazamir/

Hazamir, the National Jewish High School Choir, travels to Israel to tour and sing. The group has outposts throughout the mid-Atlantic states and Boston. If you're a teenager and you like to sing, or travel, or both, be sure to check the Teenagers chapter for more listings on each topic.

Inward Bound

http://www.solon.com/~ib/bwca/bwcamain.html

Inward Bound, the brainchild of a Lubavitch rabbi in Minnesota, offers small group hiking and camping trips with a Jewish flavor in places like Yosemite, Costa Rica, and of course Israel. With links to Minnesota Moishe's Favorite Fishing Spots.

Israel, with the Jews of Anchorage

http://www.alaska.net/~sholom/israel.html

Travel to Israel with the Jews of Anchorage, Alaska's Congregation Beth Sholom.

Jerusalem One—Israel

http://www.jer1.co.il/siteindex/indextra.htm

Websites for a decent number of Israeli hotels, kibbutzim, and travel opportunities. From Jerusalem One. There really isn't a single commercial provider of Israeli travel information that competes with a guidebook. At least not yet, anyway.

Jewish Singles Vacations

http://www1.usa1.com/~coatnet/jsv/

If you're between the ages 30 and 49, you can learn about trips to Hawaii, Europe, and beyond. You'll find itineraries and photos, and you can register online.

Lonely Planet

http://www.lonelyplanet.com/letters/meast/isr_pc.htm

Hip travel tips from readers of the Lonely Planet guide to travel in Israel. For example: Never cross the border to Egypt after 3 P.M., writes Mark Yoffe of the U.S. The buses stop running, he reports, and the cabbies will rip you off. And Zsolt Kispal of Hungary says that you can find "casual work" in Tel Aviv if you run low on funds. He advises against taking high-paying (15 shekels an hour) jobs: "You can expect to work so hard that you will be dying the day after." Let's keep in mind, though, that his basis of comparison is Eastern Europe. Now, please, that was just a joke, okay?

Here's a travel tip of my own: If you take only one trip a year, you should get out more often.

Passover in Cannes, France

http://ourworld.compuserve.com:80/homepages/normm/

Looking for a change this Passover? How about spending Passover in Cannes, France? Pourquoi is this nuit not like the other nuits, eh, ma cherie? The trip is sponsored by the Beit Din, or rabbinical court, of Paris. You'll find details and photos here.

Physicians in Israel

http://www1.usa1.com/~apf/israel_tour.html

Medical professionals may find interesting trips to Israel that combine sightseeing with medical seminars. Sponsored by the American Physicians Fellowship for Medicine in Israel.

Poland

http://www.kks.com/pj/other6.html

Travel to Poland with the Project Judaica Foundation and study pre-Holocaust Eastern European Jewish communities. Jointly sponsored with New York University. The website offers information about the trip and links up with a boutique selling rather expensive Judaica.

Programs for Students in Israel

http://www.rpi.edu/~mandes/Israel_Programs.html

Here's an extensive collection of information about study programs in Israel, from Shai Israel Mandel. Topics include "A Concise Guide to Israel Programs"; summer programs; creative arts programs; volunteer opportunities/programs; higher education in Israel; ulpanim (intensive Hebrew schools for adults); and yeshivot.

Tel Dor Expedition

http://www.qal.berkeley.edu/~teldor/

Join the archeologists of the University of California at Berkeley as they continue their Tel Dor excavations in Israel. (Be sure to see the Archeology chapter too.)

CHAPTER FORTY-ONE

VIDEO AND FILM

THIS AREA OF THE JEWISH INTERNET is certain to explode as online video technology becomes easier to use and less expensive. The sites reviewed offer ideas on innovative uses of the Net—specifically, allowing you to view film and video clips right on your computer screen. Hollywood currently offers previews of some big-budget films on the Net; car companies like Ford let you spin the exteriors of new models. Jewish filmmakers and video artists can reach massive new audiences; show clips; introduce film festivals; provide reviews; find actors, crew, screenwriters, subjects, financiers, distribution... the possibilities are endless. The pickings, for now, are slim, but that's likely to change rapidly.

Films and Theater by and About Jewish Women

http://world.std.com/~alevin/film.html

Brief descriptions and availability of films by and about Jewish women. Yiddish theater and television are described here, too. Films from Israel, the U.S., Mexico, France, Germany, and elsewhere.

Israel Film Festival in New York and Los Angeles

http://www.bway.net/israel/index.html

Visit this website to learn about the films, the filmmakers, the symposia, Israfest, and everything else concerned with the Israel Film Festival on the left and right coasts. Have your server call my server, and we'll do lunch.

Jewish Film Programmers Worldwide

http://www.well.com/user/ari/jff/worldwide.html

Filmmakers and lovers of film will find useful this worldwide address list of Jewish film festivals. You'll find festivals from Chicago to Copenhagen, Brussels to Baltimore.

Jewish Video Competition

http://www.slip.net/~jewvideo/

Learn about this Jewish video competition, sponsored by the Judah L. Magnes Museum in Berkeley, California.

List of Jewish Films and Videos

http://members.aol.com/jewfilm/index.html#Strange

This site lists a large number of films, many with links to their home pages. Of particular interest to those researching the history of Jewish film and the image of Jews and Judaism as presented on film.

Moriah Films

http://www.wiesenthal.com/moriah/

Moriah Films, a project of the Simon Wiesenthal Center in Los Angeles, specializes in documentary filmmaking that reinforces human rights while offering Jewish perspectives. Their first co-production is *Liberation*, a documentary that intertwines the story of the Allied invasion with Hitler's attempt to destroy the Jews. Find out more about Moriah Films and their current projects at their site.

Shtetl: A Film by Marian Marzynski

http://www.clarityconnect.com/webpages/grunberg/shtetl.html

Visit this interesting website to learn all about filmmaker Marian Marzynski's film *Shtetl—A Journey Home*, which tells the story of Jewish-Polish relations past and present through the eyes of a 70-year-old Jewish Chicagoan as he revisits his Polish birthplace of Bransk. You can even download and read the script for this film.

South Bay Jewish Film Series

http://www.best.com/~sbjfs/index.shtml

The Los Gatos, California, Jewish community offers their South Bay Jewish Film Series. Other Jewish groups thinking of creating or expanding a film series ought to check this one out for excellent ideas. You'll also find an "ever growing" alphabetical listing of Jewish movies giving titles, country of origin, year, and type, for hundreds of Jewish films. You can search the list by topic (comedy, Holocaust, etc.). This would be fantastic if it were annotated. You'll also find links to Jewish film festivals across North America and the world.

The Steven Spielberg Film Archive   RECOMMENDED

http://www2.huji.ac.il/www_jcj/jfa.html

The Steven Spielberg Jewish Film Archive at Hebrew University of Jerusalem comprises the world's largest collection of Jewish/Israeli documentary film material. Most of the films were shot in Israel and include newsreels from 1935-1971; videotapes of the Eichmann trial; the collection of the Ghetto Fighters' Museum; and archives of organizations and government offices from all over Israel. Regular users of the Archive include filmmakers and news producers from all over the world. Read the newsletter, learn more about the Archive, or find out how you can use it from anywhere on the planet.

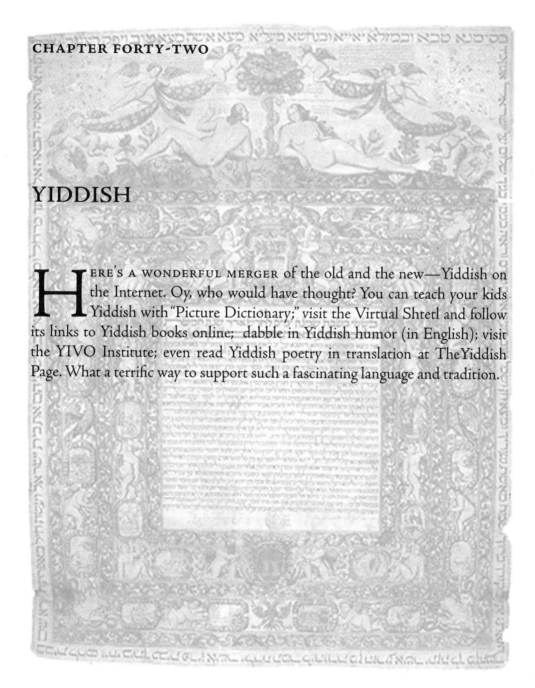

CHAPTER FORTY-TWO

YIDDISH

ERE'S A WONDERFUL MERGER of the old and the new—Yiddish on the Internet. Oy, who would have thought? You can teach your kids Yiddish with "Picture Dictionary," visit the Virtual Shtetl and follow its links to Yiddish books online; dabble in Yiddish humor (in English); visit the YIVO Institute; even read Yiddish poetry in translation at The Yiddish Page. What a terrific way to support such a fascinating language and tradition.

Australia: J. Waks Cultural Centre

http://www.ozemail.com.au/~mzylberm/

Yiddish culture down under: The J. Waks Community Centre of Melbourne, Australia, seeks to promote Yiddish culture. Learn about them here and find links to other Melbourne Yiddish groups, like the KOALA Farlag. Now that's *taka* a name. If you don't know what *taka* means, ask your *zaide*. If you don't know what *zaide* means, ask your *bubbe*.

Boston's Yiddish Voice

http://world.std.com/~yv/

Program notes, archives, sound recordings, and links to other Yiddish resources at the site of Boston's leading Yiddish radio program, the Yiddish Voice. When last I visited I was treated to a recording of Sholom Aleichem reading from "If I Were Rothschild [a rich man]."

Chaya Rochel Andres: The Years Have Sped By   RECOMMENDED

http://www.ncc.com:80/dvjcc/Yiddish/contents.html

This is a moving and beautifully written autobiography in English and Yiddish of Chaya Rochel Andres, a poet, a Holocaust survivor, and member of the Dallas, Texas, Jewish community. She alone among her family members survived Hitler, because she ran away to escape an unwanted marriage. An admirable use of the Internet, from the Dallas Virtual Jewish Commuity Center.

Hebrew and Yiddish Texts

http://www.cs.engr.uky.edu/~raphael/yiddish.html

These texts of lyrics and poetry come to you as graphics files in GIF (graphic information file) format, which means that you don't need any special fonts to view the Hebrew and Yiddish on your computer. Still, you will need to know how to read Hebrew and Yiddish, because these texts are not translated. This site would be a heck of a lot more useful if the provider gave some information about the pieces and their authors or composers.

RECOMMENDED

The *Jewish Forward*

http://www.forward.com/

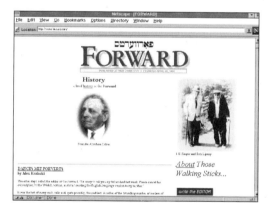

The *Jewish Forward*, the leading Yiddish-speaking newspaper in the world, welcomed hundreds of thousands of Jewish immigrants to America and now welcomes you to its sparkling home page. Besides a history of the *Forward*, you'll find news from 90, 75, and 50 years ago, as well as current news, features, and graphics that make this site well worth your visit.

Picture Dictionary

RECOMMENDED

http://shamash.nysernet.org/computers/rtls-software/aryeh2z.html

Teach your kids Yiddish with this downloadable, shareware Hebrew/Yiddish/English Picture Dictionary. It's adorable.

Poetry of Menke Katz

http://members.aol.com/thesmith1/menke.html

Menke Katz made his mark in literature as a poet in both Yiddish and English. Meet him and order his works here.

Virtual Shtetl

http://sunsite.unc.edu/yiddish/shtetl.html

Virtual Shtetl, the Yiddish Language and Culture Home Page, includes a library, synagogue, school, kitchen, memorial, art center, and other resources. Each links to related sites: The Library has links to Yiddish books and bibliographies online; the Kitchen takes you to recipes; and Memorial takes you to online Holocaust-related resources. Click on Library and the Dictionaries and you'll find a list of the 123 Yiddish words that made their way into the Oxford English Dictionary (as the rest of us kvell with pride).

"What the Chelm?"

http://waldorf.cc.wwu.edu:2501/chelmhome.html

This website is listed as "What the Chelm?" Chelm, of course, is the fictional town in the Yiddish stories of, um, great Yiddish authors. So I click on it and Netscape immediately replies, "No information in file."

Why am I not surprised? All right, class, your assignment: Construct the website for the Jewish community of Chelm. You have one hour. Or two. Take the whole afternoon.

Yiddish Humor

http://www.bu.edu/~aarondf/fortunes.html#NAIMAN

Yiddish humor, in English, from Arthur Naiman's *Every Goy's Guide to Yiddish*. A sample: "The only ailment chicken soup can't cure is neurotic dependence on one's mother."

Yiddish Language Archive

http://world.std.com/~yv/mendele-brochurele.html

A Yiddish language and literature archive. You can upload your own articles into the database or search for information about anything to do with Yiddish culture.

The Yiddish Page

http://www.cs.brandeis.edu/~hhelf/yiddish.html

The Yiddish Page features a poem of the week transliterated and translated. When I visited, the poem was "In Winter's Dusk" by David Hofshteyn (1889-1952), translated by Robert Friend. It began, "Russian fields on winter evenings!/Where can one be more lonely, where can one be more lonely...." That's a Yiddish sensibility, wouldn't you agree?

YIVO

RECOMMENDED

http://www.ort.org/communit/yivo/start.htm

YIVO, founded in 1925, is the world's preeminent research center for Eastern European Jewish affairs. They "get" what the Internet can do, and they are in the process of posting photos, sound recordings, archival material, and more.

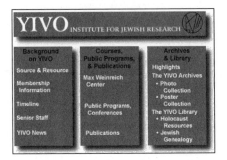

INDEX

ABOUT THE SOFTWARE AND
HOW TO INSTALL IT

To use the software you will need Microsoft Windows 3.1 or later and a Web browser (like Netscape, Microsoft Internet Explorer, Mosaic, or those that come with America Online or Prodigy).

The disk that accompanies *The Guide to the Jewish Internet* contains the Electronic Guide to the Jewish Internet and all the Hebrew fonts you need to read Hebrew with your Web browser. But before you can use the software, you need to install it.

If you don't have an Internet connection or a Web browser, call one of the companies below and ask them for their free startup offer:

America Online (1-888-265-8002)

CompuServe (1-800-848-8199)

Netcom (1-800-638-2661)

Prodigy (1-800-776-3449)

Or, check your local computer magazines for Internet service providers—companies that offer Internet connection service—in your area. (You'll usually need to provide your own browser, like Netscape or Internet Explorer.)

Installing The Electronic Guide
to the Jewish Internet

To install the software, begin at the MS-DOS prompt. To reach the MS-DOS prompt, do the following:

Windows 3.1 Exit Windows. You'll know that you've reached MS-DOS when you see a black screen and C:\> with a blinking cursor.

Windows 95 Click on the Start button, scroll up to Programs, and then select MS-DOS Prompt. You'll know that you've reached MS-DOS when you see a black screen with C:\> and a blinking cursor.

Once you see the MS-DOS prompt, insert the *The Electronic Guide to the Jewish Internet* disk in your floppy disk drive (designated either A: or B:), type either **A:** or **B:** at the prompt, and press Enter. You should now see either A:\> or B:\> on your screen. Now type **LETSGO** at the blinking cursor and press Enter to start the installation program. Instructions will appear on your screen to take you step by step through the installation program. Depending on your system, you may use your mouse or the arrow and Enter keys on your keyboard to make selections during installation. When installation is complete, the message "Installation complete" will appear on your screen.

To return to Windows:

If you're using Windows 3.1, type **WIN**

If you're using Windows 95, type **EXIT**

During the installation process, the program creates a new directory folder in your computer named "Jewish" and copies all of the files from the floppy to that folder. Installation also creates the following sub-directories inside the Jewish folder: Hebrew fonts can be found under "Webfonts"; "Guide" contains the Electronic Guide to the Jewish Internet; and "Images" contains various images used in the Electronic Guide. Once you've run the installation program and these files are copied to your computer, you will *not* need to repeat this process with the disk when you want to use the software. You can simply open these files from your Web browser.

Using the Guide to the Jewish Internet
with Web Browsers

The instructions for using the Electronic Guide are all basically the same for the major Web browsers (e.g. America Online, Internet Explorer, Netscape, or Prodigy): After installing the software, start your Web browser and double-click on the file **start_me.htm**, which you'll find in the (newly created) c:\jewish directory.

The start_me.htm file contains the hyperlinked table of contents for *The Guide to the Jewish Internet*. Once you're connected to the Internet and the file start_me.htm is open in your Web browser, click on the chapter title that contains the sites you're interested in and then click on a website's address to visit it. You can use this file either as a companion to the book (read the book and then visit the sites that catch your eye), or use the file alone to browse. Here are some specifics for the different browsers:

NOTE: Depending on your system, starting the Electronic Guide may be quite simple. Before trying any of the steps below, try clicking on the file **start_me.htm** from within either File Manager (Windows 3.1) or Explorer (Windows 95) to see if it opens automatically in your Web browser. If not, follow the procedures outlined for your system.

America Online

Connect to America Online and click on the Internet button. Click on The Web button at the next screen to launch America Online's Web browser. When the Web browser is running, choose File and then Open from the menu bar at the top of your screen. Locate start_me.htm (in c:\jewish) in the dialog box and double-click on it to open it. Click on the highlighted links to cruise from site to site. Use the Back button (or click on the links marked "Return to Table of Contents") to return to where you began. To return to your home page, click on the Home button at the top of the screen.

CompuServe

Connect to CompuServe. Choose File and then Open Local File. Locate start_me.htm (in c:\jewish) in the dialog box and double-click on it to open it. Click on the highlighted links to cruise from site to site. Use the Back button (or click on the links marked "Return to Table of Contents") to return to where you began. To return home, click on the Home button.

Internet Explorer

Launch Internet Explorer and connect to the Internet. Choose Open from the File menu and type c:\jewish\start_me.htm into the box that appears and press Enter. Click on the highlighted links to cruise from site to site. Use the Back button (or click on the links marked "Return to Table of Contents") to return to where you began. To return home, click on the Home button on the toolbar at the top of the screen.

Netcom's NetCruiser

Connect to Netcom, start NetCruiser's Web browser, and choose Open WWW File from the File menu. Locate start_me.htm (in c:\jewish) in the dialog box and double-click on it to open it. Click on the highlighted links to cruise from site to site. Use Net-Cruiser's Back button (or click on the links marked "Return to Table of Contents") to return to where you began. To return home, click on the Home button.

Netscape

Launch Netscape. Choose File from the menu bar and then select Open File. Locate start_me.htm (in c:\jewish) in the dialog box and double-click on it to open it. Click on the highlighted links to cruise from site to site. Use the Back button (or click on the links marked "Return to Table of Contents") to return to where you began. To return home, click on the Home button.

Prodigy

Connect to Prodigy. Choose File from the menu bar and then select Open Local Document. Locate start_me.htm (in c:\jewish) in the dialog box and double-click on it to open it. Click on the highlighted links to cruise from site to site. Use the Back button (or click on the links marked "Return to Table of Contents") to return to where you began. To return home, click on the Home button.

Things Change ...

The Internet is a very, very active place. Although we've done our best to make sure the website addresses (URLs) that you find in both the Electronic Guide and in this book are as up-to-date as possible, we cannot guarantee that sites you want to visit haven't moved or disappeared. Many of the people who post Web pages do so through their companies or though personal accounts on services like America Online, CompuServe, or Prodigy (you can tell by the addresses—websites on America Online have "AOL" in them; websites on company accounts have the company name somewhere, like www.ibm.com, and so on).

So what to do? If you encounter such a situation, cruise on over to one of the many search engines on the Internet and type in the name of the site that you're looking for. We recommend Alta Vista (http://www.altavista.digital.com), Yahoo (http://www.yahoo.com), Excite (http://www.excite.com), and InfoSeek (http://www.infoseek.com). If this search fails, try working back up through the URL in layers. For example, if the URL you were trying to find was http://www.nostarch.com/welcome/visit.htm, and you can't find the site, try http://www.nostarch.com/welcome (leave off one layer— the "visit.htm" part in this case). But be sure when you remove layers that you do so completely. For example, don't just cut off the ".htm" part—work back to the next "/".

Another alternative is to try our website for *The Guide to the Jewish Internet* at http://www.nostarch.com/jewish. We'll post updates to links as we become aware of them. And if you do find a broken link, please tell us—send us an e-mail at jewish@nostarch.com.

Happy cruising!

Installing the Hebrew Fonts

The **LETSGO** installation program copies the following Hebrew fonts to a directory on your hard disk called c:\jewish\webfonts.

ElroNet Monospace [elronm.ttf]—monospace (fixed-width) font

ElroNet Proportional [elronp.ttf]—proportional font

Netextpro [ntxtpro.ttf]—proportional font

Netextmo [ntxtmon.ttf]—monospace (fixed-width) font

Web Hebrew AD [wehad.ttf]—proportional font

Web Hebrew Monospace [wehm.ttf]—monospace (fixed-width) font

NOTE: There are two kinds of each font—proportional and monospace—and **you should use the fonts in matching pairs.** Each pair looks different, so try each one to see which you prefer.

Before you can use the fonts with your Web browser, you need to install them as follows:

Windows 3.1 Double-click on the Main icon in Program Manager, then, as they appear, the Control Panel icon, and the Fonts icon. Now click on the Add button. At the bottom of the Add Fonts box, select C: from the Drives menu. Make sure that the "Copy fonts to Windows directory" box is checked. Now double-click on the C:\ folder icon in the Folders menu on the same screen. Once inside the C:\ folder, double-click on the Jewish folder and then double-click on the Webfonts folder. A list of six Hebrew fonts should now appear inside the List of Fonts menu. Click on the Select All button to highlight all fonts, then click on OK. When you're done, close the Control Panel and close Windows 3.1 and restart. If the fonts installed correctly you should see them listed in the Control Panel/Fonts folder. They are now ready for use.

Windows 95 Click on the Start button, scroll up to the Settings menu and select Control Panel. Once in Control Panel, double-click on the Fonts icon and choose Install New Font from the File menu. In the Add Fonts dialog box select C: from the Drives menu and make sure that the "Copy fonts to fonts folder" box is checked. Double-click on the C:\ in the Folders menu, then double-click on the Jewish folder. Find the Webfonts folder and double-click on it. A list of six Hebrew fonts should now appear in the List of Fonts menu. Click on the Select All button to highlight all fonts, then click on OK. Your new Hebrew fonts should appear in your Fonts folder. Now close all folders and close and restart Windows 95. The six Hebrew fonts are now ready for use.

Teach Your Browser to Read Hebrew

Once you've installed the Hebrew fonts, you need to teach your Web browser to use them. Here's what we know about doing this with these major Web browsers. If your browser isn't covered here, please contact the company or service directly for support.

NOTE: Even with Hebrew fonts installed, you will be able to view all English sites normally, although the type may look a bit odd.

America Online

At this writing and to our knowledge, America Online's Web browser does not allow you to read Hebrew on the Web. However, if you follow America Online's directions for using Netscape with your America Online connection (go to keyword WWW Help), you'll be able to view Hebrew Web pages through Netscape, following the instructions given later in this section.

Internet Explorer

Launch Internet Explorer and connect to the Internet. Select the View menu and select Options. On the General tab, click on the fonts you wish to use in both the Proportional Font (ElroNet Proportional, Netextpro, or Web Hebrew AD) and Fixed-Width Font (ElroNet Monospace, Netextmo, or Web Hebrew Monospace) boxes. Choose OK when complete.

Netcom's NetCruiser

Launch Netcruiser's Web browser. Choose the Settings menu and, from that menu, choose WWW Options. Click on the word "Fonts." Replace the fonts as follows: Normal, List, and Address with a Hebrew proportional font (ElroNet Proportional, Netextpro, or Web Hebrew AD); Preformatted and FTP List with a Hebrew monospace font (ElroNet Monospace, Netextmo, or Web Hebrew Monospace). Click on "OK" when you are finished.

Netscape

Start Netscape. Click on Options from the top menu bar, choose General Preferences, and click on the Fonts tab.

NOTE: Netscape uses Times New Roman as the "current proportional font" and Courier New as the "fixed font." (You may wish to return to these after you've finished reading Hebrew.) If these fonts show up on the Fonts tab, do nothing. If you happen to have other fonts listed, write down whatever font names appear so that you may return to them if you wish.

Click on the Choose Font button next to Use the Proportional Font. In the dialog box that appears, choose any one of the three proportional fonts (ElroNet Proportional, Netextpro, or Web Hebrew AD) and click on it. Choose OK. Next, click on the Choose Font button on the line below, next to Use the Fixed Font. In the dialog box that appears, choose the monospace font (ElroNet Monospace, Netextmo, or Web Hebrew Monospace) that pairs with the proportional font you just chose and click on it. Click on OK. To return to your original fonts, follow the same steps as outlined above but choose Times New Roman as your proportional font and Courier New as your fixed font.

Prodigy

Launch Prodigy's Web browser. Choose Options from the menu bar and then click on Text Styles. With "Normal Text" showing in the Element box, click on the Font button. Replace Times New Roman with one of the proportional Hebrew fonts (ElroNet Proportional, Netextpro, or Web Hebrew AD). When asked whether you want to apply this same font to other elements, choose Yes. Next, click in the Element box and choose "Preformatted." Replace Courier with a Hebrew monospace font (ElroNet Monospace, Netextmo, or Web Hebrew Monospace). Choose Save Scheme and name the new type scheme "Hebrew Fonts." Choose OK. You can switch between your original Web Browser Default scheme and your Hebrew Fonts by clicking on Options, choosing Text Styles, and then picking the appropriate scheme.

Now, Test Your Browser

Assuming that you've encountered no problems with the directions above, you should now be ready to read Hebrew on the Web. The process will happen automatically when you dial into a Web page that uses Hebrew. But how about a test? Try connecting to one of the following Hebrew sites to see if everything is working. If not, try repeating the font installation for your specific browser. If you're still having problems, please contact your online service or Internet provider for further assistance.

http://www.bezeq.co.il/   Bezek, the Israeli telephone company

http://www.coop.co.il/   A Co-op supermarket

http://www.ibm.net.il/ibm/ibmhome_heb.html   IBM Israel

http://www1.snunit.k12.il/snunit/manchi.html   The Snunit teachers network

For more information about the software included with this book, read "About the Software and How to Install It" on page 331

NOTE: For Macintosh software, help with the LETSGO installation program, or to replace defective disks, please contact No Starch Press at 401 China Basin St., Ste. 108, San Francisco, CA 94107-2192; tel.: 415/284-9900; fax: 415/284-9955; E-mail: info@nostarch.com; http://www.nostarch.com.